Wit

Rides Again

Humorous quotation books from Prion

Des MacHale
Wit
Wit Hits The Spot
(previously entitled More Wit)
Wit on Target
(previously entitled Yet More Wit)
Wit — The Last Laugh
Ultimate Wit

Aubrey Dillon Malone
The Cynic's Dictionary

Stephen Robins
The Importance of Being Idle
How to be a Complete Dandy
The Ruling Asses — a little book of political stupidity

Michelle Lovric
Women's Wicked Wit

Rosemary Jarski
Wisecracks — Great lines from the Hollywood movies
Hollywood Wit — Classic off-screen quips and quotes

Wit
Rides Again

Des MacHale

PRION

Published in 2001 by
Prion Books Ltd.,
Imperial Works, Perren Street,
London NW5 3ED

First published 2000
Reprinted 2002

A catalogue record of this book can be obtained
from the British Library

ISBN 1–85375–436–6

Printed and bound in Great Britain by
Creative Print & Design Ltd., south Wales

Contents

Introduction

The publishers, in a desperate but futile attempt to put a halt to my gallop, called my previous book in this series *Wit: The Last Laugh*. But I am not to be denied, so *Wit Rides Again*, folks, as volume five of what is now surely the world's greatest ever collection of witty quotes, culled from every source imaginable and numbering almost ten thousand items in all. And don't take my word for it that the standard of *Wit* is not flagging: read the quotes for yourself and see how long you can continue, doubled up, helpless with laughter.

The time has come for me to nominate those men and women whom I regard as the greatest wits of all time. They are a diverse lot: comedians, humorists, essayists, novelists, poets, philosophers, sitcom stars, politicians and lots of other things, but they have one thing in common: they have all produced top-class quotable wit, and, this is important, in considerable volume. These people are some of the greatest geniuses and benefactors that the human race has produced and yet they have received scant recognition from those who dish out awards. How many great wits have received the Nobel Prize for literature, an Oscar or an Emmy for a comic performance? Well, Shaw and Churchill made it, for all the wrong reasons, but not a lot of others I can think of. Anyway, here is my list of the hundred greatest wits of all time, about which I have pondered for many moons. For simplicity, I have interpreted "wit" in the widest possible sense and I have put the names in alphabetical order, because to achieve an order of merit on this scale would be well-nigh impossible.

George Ade, Dave Allen, Fred Allen, Gracie Allen, Woody Allen, Rowan Atkinson, Tallulah Bankhead, Nancy Banks-Smith, Mike Barfield, Roseanne Barr, Dave Barry, Samuel Beckett, Thomas Beecham, Max Beerbohm, Brendan Behan, Robert Benchley, Alan Bennett, Jeffrey Bernard, Yogi Berra, Ambrose Bierce, Josh Billings, Jasmine Birtles, Erma Bombeck, Jo Brand, Roy Brown, George Burns, Winston Churchill, Jilly Cooper, Tommy Cooper, Noel Coward,

Quentin Crisp, Rodney Dangerfield, Phyllis Diller, Tommy Docherty, Ken Dodd, W.C. Fields, W.S. Gilbert, A.A. Gill, Samuel Goldwyn, Dick Gregory, Lewis Grizzard, Jack Handey, Heinrich Heine, Alfred Hitchcock, Bob Hope, Edgar Howe, Kin Hubbard, Samuel Johnson, Garrison Keiller, Ann Landers, Ring Lardner, Stephen Leacock, Denis Leary, Fran Lebowitz, Hugh Leonard, Oscar Levant, Victor Lewis-Smith, Geoffrey Madan, Groucho Marx, Jackie Mason, H.L. Mencken, Paul Merton, Spike Milligan, J.B. Morton, H.H. Munro, Flann O'Brien, P.J. O'Rourke, Dorothy Parker, S.J. Perelman, Emo Philips, J.B. Priestley, Dan Quayle, Joan Rivers, Will Rogers, Rita Rudner, Damon Runyon, Mort Sahl, Alexei Sayle, Jerry Seinfeld, George Bernard Shaw, John Simon, Sydney Smith, Yakov Smirnoff, Jonathan Swift, Dylan Thomas, James Thurber, Herbert Beerbohm Tree, Lee Trevino, Mark Twain, Peter Ustinov, Auberon Waugh, Evelyn Waugh, Ruby Wax, Mae West, Katharine Whitehorn, Oscar Wilde, P.G. Wodehouse, Alexander Woollcott, Steven Wright, Henny Youngman.

And how about a top twenty? This is a very personal choice, involving some heart-rending decisions, but I could not omit any of the following: Woody Allen, Dave Barry, Thomas Beecham, Brendan Behan, Jeffrey Bernard, Ambrose Bierce, Roy Brown, Winston Churchill, Noel Coward, Quentin Crisp, Phyllis Diller, W.C. Fields, Spike Milligan, Emo Philips, Joan Rivers, Rita Rudner, Jerry Seinfeld, Mark Twain, Oscar Wilde, Steven Wright.

There are many, many others on the fringes who would feature in other people's lists and I would be delighted to see the corresponding lists of any interested readers. Do enjoy this collection.

Des MacHale
Cork

Art

Art

I sculpt by choosing a block of marble and chopping off
anything that doesn't look like what I am trying to create.
Auguste Rodin

Art needed Ruskin like a moving train needs one of the
passengers to shove it.
Tom Stoppard

When I get to Heaven I mean to spend a considerable
portion of my first million years in painting, and so get to the
bottom of the subject.
Winston Churchill

The one unforgivable sin in art is to muddle Monet and
Manet.
Andrew McEvoy

Sister Wendy is to art what Saint Teresa was to sex education.
A.A. Gill

Of course I can draw Von Hindenberg: I can piss the old boy
in the snow.
Max Liebermann

I do not paint a portrait to look like the subject, rather does
the person grow to look like his portrait.
Salvador Dali

Renoir's later work was like pastel-coloured sneezes.
David Carritt

Pictures deface more walls than they decorate.

Frank Lloyd Wright

His work was that curious mixture of bad painting and good intentions that always entitles a man to be called a representative British artist.

Oscar Wilde

I simply refuse to countenance paintings that do not have at least a horse, gladioli or a canal in them.

Dylan Moran

I see Jim Morrison's ejaculation as art while he sees it as poetry.

Linda Ashcroft

It is amazing that you can win the Turner Prize with an E in A-level art, twisted imagination and a chainsaw.

Damien Hirst

It's not hard to understand modern art. If it hangs on a wall it's a painting, and if you can walk around it, it's a sculpture.

Simon Updike

When I hear the word culture, I take out my chequebook.

Jean-Luc Goddard

You can't control life: only art you can control. Art and masturbation. Two areas in which I am expert.

Woody Allen

All architecture is great architecture after sunset.
G.K. Chesterton

If you threw every single painting made by a woman into the Atlantic, the only complaint would be that, along with a lot of futile dross, a few pretty boudoir things were gone.
Brian Sewell

If Whistler were not a genius, he would be the most ridiculous man in Paris.
Hilaire Degas

I hate flowers: I paint them because they're cheaper than models and they don't move.
Georgia O'Keeffe

In the afterlife, I wouldn't mind turning into a vermilion goldfish.
Henri Matisse

A Test match is like a painting. A one-day match is like a Rolf Harris painting.
Ian Chappell

Van Gogh became a painter because he had no ear for music.
Nikki Harris

"What are you painting?" I asked him. "Is it the Heavenly Child?" "No," he said, "it is a cow."
Stephen Leacock

4

Art

This young man is an artist. The other day I saw him in the
street in a brown jacket.

Quentin Crisp

A woman is fascinated not by art but by the noise made by
those in the field.

Anton Chekhov

The Shakespeare Memorial Theatre, Stratford-upon-Avon, is
a courageous and partly successful attempt to disguise a
gasworks as a racquets court.

Peter Fleming

Paul Klee's pictures seem to resemble, not pictures, but a
sample book of patterns of linoleum.

Cyril Asquith

My friend has chicken pox. He's running a high
temperature and his chest looks like a bad Matisse.

Noel Coward

We gotta be out of this joint, the Louvre, in twenny minutes.

Darryl F. Zanuck

For a successful exhibition, you've got to have two out of
death, sex and jewels.

Roy Strong

When it comes to ruining paintings, he's an artist.

Samuel Goldwyn

Art

I'm a bad Catholic. It's the religion of all great artists.
Brendan Behan

I would never have taken up painting if women did not have breasts.
Pierre Auguste Renoir

Paul Gauguin is a decorator tainted with insanity.
Kenyon Cox

Skill without imagination is craftsmanship and gives us many useful objects such as wickerwork and picnic baskets. Imagination without skill gives us modern art.
Tom Stoppard

Toulouse-Lautrec's favourite part of the female body was the nose. That was only natural, because when he looked up at a woman it was the first thing he saw.
Andrea Love

An American artist is the unwanted cockroach in the kitchen of a frontier society.
John Sloan

There is nothing so terrible as the pursuit of art by those who have no talent.
Somerset Maugham

Business and Money

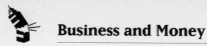

Business and Money

The trickle-down theory of economics is the less than elegant metaphor that if one feeds the horse enough oats, some will pass through to the road for the sparrows.

J. K. Galbraith

I took out a big life insurance policy because I want to be rich when I die.

Yogi Berra

Bankruptcy is a legal proceeding in which you put your money in your pants pocket and give your coat to the creditors.

Joey Adams

To the Bank of Scotland I bequeath my testicles, because it has no balls.

Lord Erskine

Don't spend two pounds to dry-clean a shirt. Donate it to the Salvation Army instead. They will clean it and put it on a hanger. Then you can buy it back for fifty pence.

Jack Dee

The gambling known as business looks with austere disfavour upon the business known as gambling.

Ambrose Bierce

I was feeling very very irritable. It was that difficult time of the month when the credit card statement arrives.

Julie Walters

Business and Money

Death is the most convenient time to tax rich people.

David Lloyd-George

The son-in-law also rises.

William Goldman

It doesn't matter if you're rich or poor, as long as you've got money.

Joe E. Lewis

A cheque is the only argument I recognise.

Oscar Wilde

You can say it was a real love match. We married for money.

S.J. Perelman

I was on a basic £100,000 a year. You don't make many savings on that.

Ernest Saunders

Ladies and gentlemen, my assistant will pass the plate around, and kindly remember that I am allergic to the sound of silver.

W.C. Fields

When I was young I'd steal from the piggy banks of dear little kiddies. Fortunately, when I got older, there were some habits I didn't change.

W.C. Fields

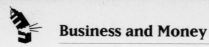

Business and Money

Jane Fonda didn't get that terrific body from exercise. She got it from lifting all that money.

Joan Rivers

Idealism is fine, but as it approaches reality, the costs become prohibitive.

William F. Buckley

There is only one thing that money can't buy and that's poverty.

Joe E. Lewis

I don't want to be a millionaire. I just want to live like one.

Walter Hagen

My boss carried only one brand of cigar. It sold for three cents. If a customer asked for a ten-cent cigar, he was handed one which sold for three cents. "The customer is always right," my boss would say, "so never allow him to be disappointed."

W.C. Fields

I need to marry someone wealthy. I'd rather not have to turn right on entering an airplane.

Tara Palmer-Tomkinson

I like going into newsagents' shops and saying, "Excuse me, is that Mars bar for sale?" When he says "Yes," I say, "OK, I might be back later, I still have a few other ones to see."

Michael Redmond

The Act of God designation on all insurance policies means roughly that you cannot be insured for the accidents that are most likely to happen to you. If your ox kicks a hole in your neighbour's Maserati, however, indemnity is instantaneous.

Alan Coren

So, Debbie McGee, what first attracted you to millionaire Paul Daniels?

Mrs Merton

H.G. Wells and George Bernard Shaw are opposed to capitalism but not to capital, when it adopts the form of a tidy balance in their own name at Barclay's Bank.

Finley Peter Dunne

The quickest way to become a millionaire is to borrow fivers off everyone you meet.

Richard Branson

The easiest way for your children to learn about money is not to have any.

Katharine Whitehorn

The business sense of a publisher is in inverse proportion to the wattage of the bulbs in his firm's toilets.

André Deutsch

A lot of people have asked me how short I am. Since my last divorce, I think I'm about $100,000 short.

Mickey Rooney

Once, when my mother mentioned an amount and I realised I didn't understand, she had to explain that's like three Mercedes. Then I understood.

Brooke Shields

The Inverse Midas Touch is the power possessed by some unfortunate beings today to turn everything they touch to shit.

Hugh Rawson

Alexander Hamilton started the U.S. Treasury with nothing: and that is the closest our country has ever come to being even.

Will Rogers

Anyone who believes that exponential growth can go on for ever in a finite world is either a madman or an economist.

Kenneth Boulding

A budget is an orderly system for living beyond your means.

Ambrose Bierce

Business is the art of extracting money from another man's pocket without resorting to violence.

Max Amsterdam

People keep telling us about their love affairs when what we really want to know is how much money they make and how they manage it.

Mignon McLaughlin

Don't worry if you're rich or not, as long as you can live comfortably and have everything you want.

Alexander Woollcott

The trick is not to live off the interest on one's capital, but off the interest on the interest.

Alan Clark

Nothing knits man to man like the frequent passage from hand to hand of cash.

Walter Sickert

Never lend people money; it gives them amnesia.

Soupy Sales

When I was seven at school one of my classmates told me all Jewish people were wealthy. Nice one. You know, I remember that day even now: running home excitedly to break the news to my mother and father. We spent that weekend taking up the floorboards.

Arnold Brown

He was a gentleman who was generally spoken of as having nothing a year, paid quarterly.

R.S. Surtees

I don't read the president's message in an annual report. I just look at his picture. If he's smiling too hard, I know the company's in big trouble.

Michael Thomsett

The modern city is a place for banking and prostitution and very little else.

Frank Lloyd Wright

I'm so fond of poverty. If it weren't so costly, I'd treat myself to it.

Pablo Picasso

Admiral Pound was pennywise.

Winston Churchill

A million wouldn't buy him, and I'd be one of them.

Bill Shankly

A builder's estimate is a sum of money equal to half the final cost.

Neil Collins

We had nothing to steal in our house. My uncle always said that if a burglar broke in he would leave a tip.

Jennifer Patterson

Honesty pays, but it doesn't seem to pay enough to suit some people.

Kin Hubbard

When you are too senior to work, then your work is going to meetings.

Woodrow Sears

The only way to make ends meet is to burn a candle at both ends.

Somerset Maugham

Drink and other Drugs

Drink and other Drugs

You don't buy beer, you just rent it.

W.C. Fields

What on earth was I drinking last night? My head feels like there's a Frenchman living in it.

Rowan Atkinson

Don't put any ice in my drink. It takes up too much room.

Groucho Marx

The South is dry and will stay dry. That is, everybody that is sober enough to stagger to the polls will.

Will Rogers

Put American beer back in the horse.

H. Allen Smith

My brother Brendan was the sort of man who would get a panic attack if he saw someone wearing a teetotaller's badge.

Brian Behan

There are three things in this world you can do nothing about. Getting AIDS, getting clamped, and running out of Chateau Lafite '45.

Alan Clark

Habitual teetotallers. There should be asylums for such people. But they would probably lapse into teetotalism as soon as they came out.

Samuel Butler

Drink and other Drugs

I have no objection to people smoking on my undertaking premises. It's good for business.

Alan Puxley

A total abstainer is the kind of man you wouldn't want to drink with even if he did.

George J. Nathan

I got Mark Helliger so drunk last night it took three bellboys to put me to bed.

W.C. Fields

Don't cry sonny and I'll let you smell my breath.

W.C. Fields

I'd give up smoking but I'm not a quitter.

Jo Brand

Good heavens! How marriage ruins a man! It's as demoralising as cigarettes and far more expensive.

Oscar Wilde

Kids nowadays are no sooner off the pot than they are back on again.

Stu Francis

A friend of mine belongs to Alcoholics Anonymous, but he's not a fanatic about it. He doesn't go to meetings: he just sends in the empties.

Milton Berle

Drink and other Drugs

I feel as though the Russian army has been walking over my tongue in their stockinged feet.

W.C. Fields

American beer is served cold so you can tell it from urine.

David Moulton

Yes, I do have a drinking problem: there's never enough.

Denis Thatcher

Show me a nation whose national beverage is beer and I'll show you an advanced toilet technology.

Paul Hawkins

I have had only one glass: maybe it has been refilled a few times, but it's only one glass.

Raymond George

Cocktails have all the disagreeability of a disinfectant without the utility.

Shane Leslie

What a strange paradox it is that I would be unemployable if I were teetotal.

Jeffrey Bernard

You can't be a real country unless you have a beer and an airline: it helps if you have some kind of football team, or some nuclear weapons, but at the very least you need a beer.

Frank Zappa

Drink and other Drugs

I have never been drunk, but I have often been overserved.
George Gobel

Yes madam, I am drunk and you are exceedingly ugly; but in the morning I shall be sober.
Winston Churchill

My favourite drink is a cocktail of carrot juice and whisky. I am always drunk but I can see for miles.
Roy Brown

Farrell's Bar in Brooklyn had urinals so large they looked like shower stalls for Toulouse-Lautrec.
Joe Flaherty

He was so full of alcohol, if you put a lighted wick in his mouth, he'd burn for three days.
Groucho Marx

I think this wine has been drunk before.
W.C. Fields

The cognac tasted like semi-viscous airplane fuel from the Amelia Earhart era.
Kinky Friedman

The man was a secular version of the Immaculate Conception. He became an alcoholic without ever buying a drink.
Niall Toibin

Drink and other Drugs

I have a hangover from forty-two years of drinking $185,000 worth of whisky.

W.C. Fields

Not one man who drinks beer in a beer commercial has a beer belly.

Rita Rudner

Oliver Reed was the people's piss-artist.

Jonathan Meades

I can't open wine bottles. Forty-five years of masturbation and I still don't have a muscle in my hand.

Billy Wilder

In my day fifty-eight beers between London and Sydney would have virtually classified you as a teetotaller.

Ian Chappell

It was the first weekend of Mardi Gras. The streets were packed with drunks like it was a Kennedy family reunion.

Drew Carey

There are three side effects of acid. Enhanced long-term memory, decreased short-term memory and I forget the third.

Timothy Leary

I always wake up at the crack of ice.

Joe E. Lewis

Drink and other Drugs

Nowadays smoking really does shorten your life because if you light up some non-smoker will kill you.

Gene Perrett

Martinis before lunch are like a woman's breasts. One is too few and three are too many.

John Humphrys

My boss took me out for a drink the other day. It was a unique experience. I'd never given blood before.

Gene Perrett

I'm thinking of taking up smoking. I'm going to start with patches and work my way up.

Jonathan Ross

Not only is this the first live televised war, it's also the first war ever covered by sober journalists.

P.J. O'Rourke

My father was ruined by hygiene. He used to supply sawdust to public houses. Now the days of the big spitters are over.

Brendan Behan

The medieval practice was to put mice or weasels in beer to flavour it, but it was considered sinful to do this deliberately and cruelly drown the beasts, so the English got the priest to bless the beer first. This absolved them, since the animals were going into a holy liquid.

Angela Costen

Drink and other Drugs

I spent ninety per cent of my salary on whisky and women.
The rest I wasted.

Tug McGraw

Never smoke opium. Gives you constipation. Terrible
binding effect. Have you ever seen a picture of the wretched
poet Coleridge? He smoked opium. He was green around
the gills and a stranger to the lavatory.

John Mortimer

Last week I told my wife, "A man is like wine, he gets better
with age." She locked me in the cellar.

Rodney Dangerfield

My New Year's resolution is that I intend to smoke a lot
more.

Jeremy Irons

Beer is an intoxicating golden brew that re-emerges virtually
unchanged an hour later.

Rick Bayan

I survived an overdose in Australia in the 1960s. I feel it is
really bad manners to commit suicide in someone else's
country.

Marianne Faithfull

I never had to turn to drink. It turned to me.

Brendan Behan

Education

Those who think they know it all are especially annoying to those of us who do.

Harold Coffin

Graduates are entitled to bleat B.A. after their names.

D. S. MacColl

My school report on mathematics read "Four per cent: effortlessly achieved."

Godfrey Smith

This college is neglecting football for education.

Groucho Marx

I wrote my name at the top of the page. I wrote down the number of the question, "1". After much reflection, I put a bracket round it thus: "(1)". But thereafter I could not think of anything connected with it that was either relevant or true. It was from these slender indications of scholarship that Mr. Weldon drew the conclusion that I was worthy to pass into Harrow. It was very much to his credit.

Winston Churchill

My school colours were "clear".

Steven Wright

Fifty per cent of this country's schoolchildren have I.Q.s below average. Under our education policy, we can turn that around.

John Clarke

Education

The most formidable headmaster I ever met was a headmistress. She had X-ray pince-nez and that undivided bust popularised by Queen Mary. I think she was God in drag.

Nancy Banks-Smith

Given a choice of weapons with you, sir, I would choose grammar.

Halliwell Hobbes

One legend that keeps recurring throughout history, in every culture, is the story of Popeye.

Jack Handey

All the convent taught me was that if you spit on a pencil eraser, it will erase ink.

Dorothy Parker

I hated school: arson was an option.

Alan Davies

Mamma, whose views on education are remarkably strict, has brought me up to be extremely short-sighted; it is part of her system.

Oscar Wilde

In elementary school, in case of fire, you have to line up quietly in a single file line from smallest to tallest. What is the logic? Do tall people burn slower?

Jack Handey

Fourteen years in the professor dodge have taught me that one can argue ingeniously on behalf of any theory, applied to any piece of literature. This is rarely harmful, because normally no one reads such essays.

Robert Parker

Our history master was also known to possess a pair of suede shoes, a sure sign in the Melbourne of the period of sexual ambivalence.

Barry Humphries

In this address at the beginning of the new academic year I intended to give you some advice, but now I remember how much is left over from last year unused.

George Harris

The intelligent are to the intelligentsia what a gentleman is to a gent.

Stanley Baldwin

There is much to be said in favour of modern journalism. By giving us the opinions of the uneducated, it keeps us in touch with the ignorance of the community.

Oscar Wilde

School is just a jail with educational opportunities.

Robertson Davies

I have lectured on campuses for a quarter of a century, and it is my impression that after taking a course in The Novel, it is an unusual student who would ever want to read a novel again.

Gore Vidal

When bad ideas have nowhere else to go, they emigrate to America and become university courses.

Frederic Raphael

History is just a distillation of rumour.

Thomas Carlyle

As long as there are tests, there will be prayer in public schools.

David Letterman

Colleges hate geniuses just as convents hate saints.

Ralph Waldo Emerson

I told my father I was punished in school because I didn't know where the Azores were. He told me to remember where I put things in future.

Henny Youngman

A professor at a British university can be fired for only two reasons; first, gross immorality on the office furniture (I think the floor is all right) and second and worse, pinching the tea-things.

Isaac Asimov

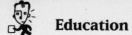

After finding no qualified candidates for the position of principal, the school board is extremely pleased to announce the appointment of David Steele to the post.

Philip Streifer

After he has served his jail sentence for perjury, Jonathan Aitken will be accepted at Oxford University to read theology. A statement from the University said: "We are satisfied that he has met the full requirements for his intended course of academic study."

Andrew Pierce

I have three A-levels: one in pure mathematics and one in applied mathematics.

Spike Milligan

I knew this girl who was a terrible speller: she worked for two years in a warehouse.

Larry Wilde

A class reunion is a meeting where three hundred people hold in their stomachs for four hours while writing down the names and addresses of friends they'll never contact.

Brenda Davidson

Instead of giving money to found colleges to promote learning, why don't they pass a constitutional amendment prohibiting anybody from learning anything? If it works as good as the Prohibition one did, in five years we would have the smartest race of people on earth.

Will Rogers

Education

Our principal writers have nearly all been fortunate in escaping regular education.

Hugh Macdiarmuid

A mother recently moaned to me that she had her Fiona tested, but sadly she wasn't dyslexic: "Oh, so she's just normal then. I am sorry."

A.A. Gill

I acquired my first motorbike, left behind by one of the masters who had to go because he had V.D.

Jennifer Patterson

There is no limit to stupidity. Space itself is said to be bounded by its own curvature, but stupidity continues beyond infinity.

Gene Wolfe

The chapter on the Fall of the Rupee you may omit. It is somewhat too sensational.

Oscar Wilde

A fool's brain digests philosophy into folly, science into superstition, and art into pedantry. Hence university education.

George Bernard Shaw

A school bus driver is someone who thought he liked children.

John Rooney

A woman who has a head full of Greek or carries on fundamental controversies about mechanics might as well have a beard.

Immanuel Kant

You didn't understand this at first, but my CONVINCING USE OF CAPITAL LETTERS HAS MADE IT ALL CLEAR TO YOU.

J. Nairn

The worst problem in the world has got to be missing children but they got the wrong people looking for those kids: the F.B.I.: and they can't find them. You got to get the Student Loan Association looking for them. I graduated from the University of Iowa nine years ago, I've moved fifty times, never left any forwarding address anywhere, I'm walking through the casino in Atlantic City and a payphone rings. It was the S.L.A.

Tom Arnold

Homework is something teenagers do during commercials.

Brenda Davidson

Eton was an early introduction to human cruelty, treachery and extreme physical hardship.

Alan Clark

The more tolerant among us regard foreign languages as a kind of speech impediment that could be overcome by willpower.

Barbara Ehrenreich

Learning has gained most by those books which the printers have lost.

Thomas Fuller

It distresses me, this failure to keep pace with the leaders of thought as they pass into oblivion.

Max Beerbohm

Why is "abbreviation" such a long word?

Steven Wright

School is where you go between when your parents can't take you and industry can't take you.

John Updike

I actually do think I'm quite intelligent. But my intelligence seems to be a different type from everyone else's.

Tara Palmer-Tomkinson

I am not an intellectual but I have this look.

Woody Allen

It is too early to form a judgement about the French Revolution.

Zhou Enlai

I have tried to know absolutely nothing about a great many things, and I have succeeded fairly well.

Robert Benchley

All I can remember about the Sociology final examination paper was that the first question was "Leave the exam hall and persuade the first passerby to accompany you through life, using irony where necessary".

Charles Goulding

Liberals have invented whole college majors: psychology, sociology, women's studies: to prove that nothing is anybody's fault.

P. J. O'Rourke

I didn't have any education so I had to use my brains.

Bill Shankly

Harold Macmillan has had an expensive education: Eton and Suez.

Harold Wilson

What did I do for my college at Oxford? I drank for it.

Evelyn Waugh

Examinations are of no value whatsoever. If a man is a gentleman, he knows quite enough, and if he is not a gentleman whatever he knows is bad for him.

Oscar Wilde

You want either a first or a fourth. There is no value in anything between. Time spent on a good second is time thrown away.

Evelyn Waugh

The ignorance of Harold Ross was an Empire State Building of ignorance. You had to admire it for its size.

Dorothy Parker

There are two kinds of medical lecture: those that contain slides and those that contain original thought.

Henry Miller

An expert is any lecturer from out of town, with slides.

Jim Baumgarten

What he lacks in intelligence, he makes up for in stupidity.

Anthony Hughes

All you need in life is ignorance and confidence and then success is assured.

Mark Twain

Food

Food

Dried fish is a staple food in Iceland: it varies in toughness.
The tougher kind tastes like toenails, and the softer kind like
the skin off the soles of one's feet.

W. H. Auden

I went into McDonald's the other day and asked for some
fries. The girl at the counter said, "Would you like some fries
with that?"

Jay Leno

Her cooking suggested that she had attained the Cordon
Noir.

Leo Rosten

One thing my mother could never say to me is that my eyes
were bigger than my belly.

Roy Brown

No Roman was ever able to say, "I dined last night with the
Borgias."

Max Beerbohm

I will never understand why they cook on TV. I can't smell
it. Can't eat it. Can't taste it. At the end of the show they
hold it up to the camera. "Well here it is. You can't have any.
Thanks for watching. Goodbye."

Jerry Seinfeld

I'd like to live on Mars.

Jo Brand

Airline food is gastronomic murder, preceded by culinary torture.

Egon Ronay

A diet is a system of starving yourself to death so you can live a little longer.

Totie Fields

The older you get, the better you get: unless you're a banana.

Rose Nylund

If you are in the process of preparing something, food licked off knives and spoons has no calories, e.g. peanut butter on a knife or spoon.

Lewis Grizzard

You seem quite out of sorts. You haven't quarrelled with your cook, I hope? What a tragedy that would be for you; you would lose all your friends.

Oscar Wilde

Whenever you get sick at a party there will always be carrots. You may never have eaten a carrot in your life, you may have led a totally carrot-free existence, but there they are, bloody carrots.

Mike Harding

Never trust a thin cook.

Charlotte Wright

Food

When drinking a diet soda while eating a candy bar, the calories in the candy bar are cancelled by the diet soda. And cookie pieces contain no calories. The process of breaking the cookie causes calorie leakage.

Lewis Grizzard

My mother is the only person in the world who cooks lumpy boiled water.

David Brenner

I live in a place called Green Lanes, but that's a misnomer. The only green you see is on a Saturday night when people are throwing up the salad off their kebabs.

Alan Davies

It is time to go on a diet when the Prudential offers you group insurance.

Totie Fields

I just love animals, especially in good gravy.

Freddie Starr

There is only one secret to bachelor cooking: not caring how it tastes.

P. J. O'Rourke

Good mashed potato is one of the great luxuries of life and I don't blame Elvis for eating it every night for the last year of his life.

Lindsey Bareham

Food

"Turbot, sir," said the waiter, placing before me two wishbones, two eyeballs and a bit of black mackintosh.
Thomas E. Welby

It has been said that fish is good brain food. That's a fallacy. But brains are good fish food.
Mel Brooks

As a child my family's menu consisted of two choices: take it or leave it.
Buddy Hackett

Coffee in England is just toasted milk.
Christopher Foy

Now all your doughnuts can be like Fanny's.
Johnny Craddock

A delicatessen is a shop selling the worst parts of animals more expensively than the nice parts.
Mike Barfield

Large, naked, raw carrots are acceptable food only to those who live in hutches eagerly awaiting Easter.
Fran Lebowitz

Why do people who work in health food shops always look so unhealthy?
Victoria Wood

Late night snacks have no calories. The refrigerator light is not strong enough for the calories to see their way into the food.

Lewis Grizzard

Colonel Sanders really dug chicks. The only things he really cared about were breasts, legs and thighs.

John Erskine

Tofu. Girls, have you ever had a yeast infection? It's not a million miles away from what tofu looks like.

Ruby Wax

If a man prepares dinner for you and the salad contains three or more types of lettuce, he is serious.

Rita Rudner

Continental breakfasts are very sparse, usually just a pot of coffee or tea and a teensy roll that looks like a suitcase handle. My advice is to go right to lunch without pausing.

Miss Piggy

I have a great diet. You're allowed to eat anything you want, but you must eat it with naked fat people.

Ed Bluestone

A fire broke out in my kitchen. The firemen arrived and put it out, but three of them had to be treated for food inhalation.

Phyllis Diller

There are food scares in Belgium involving everything from poultry to chocolate. To the despair of many worldwide, however, another millennium ends without any bad news about Brussels sprouts.

Frank McNally

I did toy with the idea of doing a cookbook. The recipes were to be the routine ones: how to make dry toast, instant coffee, hearts of lettuce and brownies. But as an added attraction, at no extra charge, my idea was to put a fried egg on the cover. I think a lot of people who hate literature but love fried eggs would buy it if the price was right.

Groucho Marx

Things that are said to do good generally taste of sawdust and burnt rubber.

R. W. Howarth

Is there no Latin word for "tea"? Upon my soul, if I had known that I would have left the vulgar stuff alone.

Hilaire Belloc

My favourite part of the body is the navel. I like to eat celery in bed and it's an excellent place to keep the salt.

Gerard Hoffnung

Sir Redvers Buller plodded from blunder to blunder and from one disaster to another, without losing either the regard of his country or the trust of his troops, to whose feeding as well as his own he paid serious attention.

Winston Churchill

In 1346 bubonic plague sees rats taken off the menu across Europe, but in an effort to shore up public confidence, Edward III insists "British rodent-meat is safe".

Frank McNally

I am a man more dined against than dining.

Maurice Bowra

Life is uncertain. Eat dessert first.

Ernestine Ulmer

Audrey Hepburn was the patron saint of anorexics.

Orson Welles

Shane Warne's idea of a balanced diet is a cheeseburger in each hand.

Ian Healy

You should tip the waiter ten dollars, minus two dollars if he tells you his name, another two dollars if he claims it will be His Pleasure to serve you and another two dollars for each "special" he describes involving confusing terms such as "shallots".

Dave Barry

Any month whose name contains the letter a, e or u is a proper time for chocolate.

Sandra Boynton

Do you know what the fourth great lie is after "The cheque's in the post" etc.? It is "I know a great Mexican restaurant." Oh no you don't.

A.A. Gill

My parents used to work for British Rail. My mother was a teabag drier and my father used to weld the crusts onto the pork pies.

Eric Morecambe

My father ate a banana with a knife and fork: to modern minds a dead give away if there ever was one.

Quentin Crisp

All dates consist of three things; food, entertainment and affection. At first, there is a lot of entertainment and only a little affection. As the relationship progresses, the entertainment is decreased and the affection is increased. When the affection becomes the entertainment, we no longer call it "dating". At no time may the food be omitted.

Judith Manners

On the train, why do I always wind up sitting next to the woman who's eating the individual fruit pie by sucking the filling out through the hole in the middle?

Victoria Wood

Eat what you like until you're five pounds overweight, then lose ten pounds. Then dear boy, start eating again.

Noel Coward

Food

I once had dinner in a topless restaurant. I was really looking forward to it. But all the staff were men.

Emo Philips

What a wonderful feast, especially the mint jelly. I loved the way it glowed in the dark.

Jeremy Clarkson

I diet between meals.

Michael Winner

I come from a family where gravy is considered a beverage.

Erma Bombeck

Most turkeys taste better the day after; my mother's tasted better the day before.

Rita Rudner

Pizza gives lie to the four food groups theory because many teenagers are still alive.

Brenda Davidson

Frogs legs. I could never order them. I keep wondering, "What do they do with the rest of the frog?" Do they give them little dollies and send them back out on the street to beg?

George Carlin

Auntie said grace in a clear authoritative voice: "O Lord, what we are about to receive, may it pass through us peacefully."

Kerr Donald

There was a café in Liverpool that used to advertise "If Colonel Sanders had chicken like ours, he would have been a General."

Tom O'Connor

A refrigerator is a place where you store leftovers until they're old enough to throw out.

Al Boliska

I eat in someone else's restaurant only if I'm thinking of buying it.

Marco Pierre White

He that but looketh on a plate of ham and eggs to lust after it, hath already committed breakfast with it in his heart.

C.S. Lewis

While the other desperate spinsters are killing and maiming each other to catch the bouquet, I'm on my way to the reception for an early plate of sausage rolls and vol-au-vents.

Jo Brand

A casserole can progress from uncooked to burnt without passing through singe.

Esther Selsdon

Food

I'd like to force-feed supermodels with chocolate éclairs and keep them tied up so they couldn't exercise. Much easier to make them look like you than try to look like them.

Jo Brand

The main principle of infant digestion is, that much of what goes in must, eventually, come out but not necessarily by the expected route.

Esther Selsdon

The lunches of fifty-seven years had caused his chest to slip down to the mezzanine floor.

P. G. Wodehouse

Foods that are frozen have no calories because calories are units of heat. Examples are ice-cream, frozen pies and Popsicles.

Lewis Grizzard

Eternity is two people and a roast turkey.

James Dent

I'm on this fantastic new diet. You eat whatever you want, whenever you want, as much as you want. You don't lose any weight, but it's really easy to stick to.

George Tricker

Lawyers and other Professions

Lawyers and other Professions

A journalist is someone who stays sober right up to lunch time.

Godfrey Smith

The judge asked me where I was in the interim. I told him I had never been near the place.

Jimmy Durante

I don't mind hecklers, because I know how to ignore people: I was an airline stewardess.

Jo-Ann Deering

You may leave the court with no other stain on your character other than the fact that you have been acquitted by an Irish jury.

Maurice Healy

A lawyer with his briefcase can steal more than a thousand men with guns.

Mario Puzo

The crime rate in Mexico City is so high because the police wear uniforms and the criminals always spot us.

Francisco Luna

Frankly, I don't believe people think of their office as a workplace anyway. I think they think of it as a stationery store with Danish. You want to get your pastry, your envelopes, your supplies, your toilet paper, six cups of coffee and you go home.

Jerry Seinfeld

Lawyers and other Professions

I read the other day of a man who was cleared of causing cruelty to animals in Maryland. The prosecution said he had had sex with a raccoon but in his defence he said the animal was dead at the time and therefore could not have suffered.

Jeremy Clarkson

I should urge your client to observe, and to ensure that his dog observes, the standards of behaviour proper to their respective levels of creation.

Geoffrey Madan

I have all the Christian virtues except that of resignation.

Lord Denning

The defendant aroused the landlord's suspicion as he was the only one in the pub wearing prison uniform.

Mick Potter

In Washington, D.C, there are more lawyers than people.

Sandra O'Connor

The firm of Batten, Barton, Durstine & Osborne sounds like a trunk falling downstairs.

Fred Allen

Epitaph on a dead waiter: By and by, God caught his eye.

David McCord

Four-fifths of the perjury in the world is expended on tombstones, women and competitors.

Lord Dewar

Lawyers and other Professions

I was a witness in a road accident case. All I could testify is that the cars hit each other at about the same time.

Steven Wright

The policeman who arrested me said I was doing between 106 and 108 miles an hour. "107 then," I said.

Alan Davies

Hijackers should be given a rapid trial with due process of law, then hanged.

Edward Davis

The main difference between O.J. Simpson and Christopher Reeves is that O.J. walked while Christopher Reeves got the electric chair.

Tim Dedopulos

The long and distressing controversy over capital punishment is very unfair to anyone contemplating murder.

Geoffrey Fisher

Nothing is more annoying than to be obscurely hanged.

Voltaire

There are many different jobs for cops these days. It seems to me that the Chalk Outline Guy is one of the better jobs you can get. It's not too dangerous, the criminals are long gone: that seems like a good one. I don't know who those guys are. I guess they're people who wanted to be sketch artists but they couldn't draw too well.

Jerry Seinfeld

Lawyers and other Professions

It is probably no mere chance that in legal textbooks the problems relating to married women are usually considered immediately after the pages devote to idiots and lunatics.

A.P. Herbert

Dorothy Parker and I once shared the tiniest office space imaginable. One cubic foot less of space and it would have constituted adultery.

Robert Benchley

They were as scarce as lawyers in heaven.

Mark Twain

With Congress, every time they make a joke it's a law and every time they make a law it's a joke.

Will Rogers

The only difference between a pigeon and a farmer today is that a pigeon can still make a deposit on a tractor.

M.E. Kerr

In America they lock up juries and let the defendants out on bail.

Herbert Prochnow

Death is one of the worst things that can happen to a Mafia member, and many prefer to pay a fine.

Woody Allen

An executive is just an ulcer with authority.

Fred Allen

Lawyers and other Professions

I don't believe that man is woman's natural enemy. Perhaps his lawyer is.

Shana Alexander

I took a job as a postman: it doesn't pay much but it's better than walking the streets.

Pat Doherty

An airplane full of lawyers was hijacked by terrorists. They threatened to release one every hour unless their demands were met.

Denis Leary

Dice are small polka-dotted cubes of ivory, constructed like a lawyer to lie on any side.

Ambrose Bierce

I'm for a stronger death penalty.

George Bush

I yield to no one in my admiration for the office as a social centre, but it is no place actually to get any work done.

Katharine Whitehorn

There is never a deed so foul that something can't be said in favour of the guy; that is why there are lawyers.

Melvin Belli

Matrimony and murder both carry a mandatory life sentence.

John Mortimer

Lawyers and other Professions

I have always found librarians close relations of the living dead.
Alan Bennett

Publishers themselves do practically no real work at all, if we exclude their digestive systems, which are always working at full pressure owing to the fact that they are always lunching and dining out. I have caught publishers doing all kinds of things: and I am afraid I cannot specify even the most innocent of them: but I have never caught a publisher working.
J.B. Priestley

A lawyer is the larval stage of a politician.
Ambrose Bierce

My only qualification for being put at the head of the Navy is that I am very much at sea.
Edward Carson

Some men are heterosexual and some men are homosexual, and some men don't think about sex at all. They become lawyers.
Woody Allen

Trial by jury is asking the ignorant to use the incomprehensible to decide the unknowable.
Hiller B. Zobel

Lawyers are really an unnecessary profession. They don't produce anything. All they do is guide you through the labyrinth of the legal system that they created: and they keep on changing it in case you start to catch on.
Ian Shoales

Lawyers and other Professions

There are so many Smiths about because Smiths were very good at picking chastity belts.

Brendan Cooper

A bad reference is almost as hard to find as a good employee.

Robert Half

I always like to compare models to supermodels in the way I compare Tampax to Super Tampax: supermodels cost a bit more and they are a lot thicker.

Jo Brand

Occasionally a lawyer sends you a legal document covered in kisses, and you really think you're getting somewhere until he tells you he only wants you to sign your name in three places.

Jilly Cooper

And it should be the law: if you use the word "paradigm" without knowing what it means, you go to jail. No exceptions.

David Jones

Crime does not pay, except for lawyer's fees.

Byron White

I do a lot of reading on serial killers: mostly *How To* books.

Roseanne Barr

He's a self-made man: the living proof of the horrors of unskilled labour.

Ed Wynn

Lawyers and other Professions

Everyone in public life should be arrested at least once. It's an education.

Alan Clark

Lawyers should never marry other lawyers. This is called inbreeding from which comes idiot children and more lawyers.

Spencer Tracy

Lawyers are an excellent source of protein.

Robin Hall

Lawyers get you out of the kind of trouble you'd never get into if there were no lawyers.

Ken Alstad

Help wanted: Telepath. You know where to apply.

Steven Wright

You cannot make a lawyer honest by an act of Congress. You've got to work on his conscience. And his lack of conscience is what made him a lawyer in the first place.

Will Rogers

The three toughest jobs are football management, lion taming and mountain rescue – in that order.

Jimmy Armfield

Literature

In the pages of Pater, the English language lies in state.

George Moore

Until twelve years ago, I didn't realise that books were translated. I thought Proust wrote in English.

Beryl Bainbridge

Last night I dined out in Chelsea and mauled the dead and rotten carcasses of several works written by my friends.

Virginia Woolf

I know I have won the Nobel Prize for literature. Stop babbling man: how much?

W. B. Yeats

Whitman was not only eager to talk about himself but reluctant to have the conversation stray from the subject for too long.

Henry D. Thoreau

There are passages of Joyce's *Ulysses* which should be read only in the toilet: if one wants to extract the full flavour of their content.

Henry Miller

It is a sad feature of modern life that only women for the most part have the time to write novels, and they seldom have much to write about.

Auberon Waugh

John Millicent Synge.

James Joyce

Metaphors be with you.

Harvey Mindess

The success of many books is due to the affinity between the mediocrity of the author's ideas and those of the public.

Sébastien Roch Nicolas Chamfort

For those sated readers of my work who ardently wish I would stop, the future looks very dark indeed.

Noel Coward

Your life would not make a good book. Don't even try.

Fran Lebowitz

I am sick and tired of obscure English towns that exist seemingly for the sole accommodation of these limerick writers: and even sicker of their residents, all of whom suffer from physical deformities and spend their time dismembering relatives at fancy dress balls.

Flann O'Brien

At certain points reading Tom Wolfe's *A Man in Full* can be said to resemble the act of making love to a 300lb woman. Once she gets on top it's all over. Fall in love, or be asphyxiated.

Norman Mailer

A magazine editor asked me if I would consider turning one of my plays into a short story for five hundred dollars. I reflected gleefully that for five hundred dollars I would gladly consider turning *War and Peace* into a music-hall sketch.

Noel Coward

Do we need another dictionary of quotations? Hell, yes! Like underpants in the Urals, you can never have enough of them.

Reginald Hill

I refused the Nobel Prize for literature on the grounds that I wish to be read by people who feel like reading my books and not by celebrity collectors.

Jean-Paul Sartre

My wife pleased me by laughing uproariously when reading my manuscript, only to inform me that it was my spelling that amused her.

Gerald Durrell

Reviewers seemed to fall into two classes: those that had little to say and those that had nothing.

Max Beerbohm

I have always been an avid reader; ever since I grew hair I could sit on, I could always be found with a torch under the sheets, until a doctor advised me to give it up and take up reading. Since then I've never looked back or up again.

Edna Everage

Life and Laughter Amidst the Cannibals relates the hilarious story of a sailor visiting the Solomon Islands who avoided being eaten by cannibals but whose false teeth fell overboard; in attempting to retrieve them, he was eaten alive by a shark.

Russell Ash

I read a book twice as fast as anybody else. First I read the beginning, then I read the ending and then I start in the middle and work towards whichever end I like best.

Gracie Allen

Everything I've said will be credited to Dorothy Parker.

George Kaufman

Here lies that peerless peer Lord Peter
Who broke the laws of God and man and metre.

John Lockhart

Balzac was so conceited that he raised his hat every time he spoke of himself.

Robert Broughton

The affair between Margot Asquith and Margot Asquith will live as one of the prettiest love stories in all literature.

Dorothy Parker

I was a genius and therefore unemployable.

Patrick Kavanagh

Literature

To hear W. B. Yeats read his own verses was as excruciating a torture as anyone could be exposed to.

Somerset Maugham

Critics are just cut-throat bandits in the paths of fame.

Robert Burns

I don't split infinitives. When I get to work on them, I break them into little pieces.

Jimmy Durante

Literary confessors are contemptible, like beggars who exhibit their sores for money, but not so contemptible as the public that buys their books.

W. H. Auden

All books over five hundred pages that weren't written by Dickens or a dead Russian are better left on the shelf.

William Blundell

I'm really into bondage. When I'm in the mood I'll tie my wife up and gag her and go into the living room and watch a football game.

Tom Arnold

There is obviously a right and a wrong time for any book and attempting as a seventeen-year-old to tackle Virginia Woolf's subtle essay in modernism, *To the Lighthouse*, on a topless beach in Biarritz was almost certainly a mistake.

Richard Beswick

I do not think I had ever seen a nastier-looking man than Percy Wyndham Lewis. Under a black hat, when I had first seen them, the eyes had been those of an unsuccessful rapist.

Ernest Hemingway

When I am asked what kind of writing is the most lucrative, I have to say, ransom notes.

H.N. Swanton

If Malcolm Hardee is as good between the covers of this book as he is between the sheets, put the book back on the shelf.

Jo Brand

Similes are like defective ammunition: the lowest thing I can think of at this time.

Ernest Hemingway

Authors should be paid by the quantity of works not written.

Jack Kirwan

Mr. Hall Caine writes at the top of his voice.

Oscar Wilde

Last thing at night I go over what I'm working on: it's the best sleeping pill.

Jilly Cooper

My father adored Shakespeare. Every time he caught sight of me he would say: "Is execution done on Cawdor?" When you are four, that's a pretty tough question.

John Mortimer

A man told me that he had been reading my works all his life. I observed that he must be very tired.

Samuel Beckett

All women poets, dead or alive, who smoke cigars, are major. All poets named Edna St. Vincent Millay are major.

E. B. White

Booksellers drink of their wine in the manner of the heroes in the hall of Odin: out of authors' skulls.

Peter Pindar

The llama is a woolly sort of fleecy hairy goat, with an indolent expression and an undulating throat like an unsuccessful literary man.

Hilaire Belloc

Oxymoron is a literary device whereby two contradictory concepts are juxtaposed: as for example in "the witty Jane Austen".

Patrick Murray

No animal was harmed in the making of this book.

Simon Rose

Publishing pays: if you don't charge for your time.

Jonathan Cape

I know everything. One has to, to write decently.

Henry James

I have given my memoirs far more thought than any of my marriages. You can't divorce a book.

Gloria Swanson

No one reads modern poetry, other than professional poets, professional poets' families, and the poetry reviewer of the *Sunday Times*.

Marcus Berkman

I always told James that he should give up writing and take up singing.

Nora Joyce

I found it impossible to work with security staring me in the face.

Sherwood Anderson

I gave my young nephew a book for Christmas. He's spent six months looking for where to put the batteries.

Milton Berle

Literature

I've just been reading the dictionary. It turns out the zebra did it.

Steven Wright

The great American novel has not only already been written, it has already been rejected.

Frank Dane

Lyric Inditer and Reciter. Poetry Promptly Executed.

W. M. McGonagall

If someone complains that punning is the lowest form of humour, you can tell them that poetry is verse.

Bob Davis

Rod McKuen's poetry is not even trash.

Karl Shapiro

When I see someone asleep over one of my books I am pleased that I have induced healthful slumber.

William M. Thackeray

Baldrick, I'd rather French kiss a skunk than listen to your poetry.

Rowan Atkinson

Poetry is so undervalued in our society that no one should be discouraged from writing it, even Jewel.

Kim Carlin

My cousin Jimmy Burke was the only one of us who could write. I mean, his name.

Brendan Behan

There comes the dreaded moment in any anthology when yours truly decides to include: himself. This fact alone is enough to condemn the book out of hand; if the anthologist cannot see the huge gap between his own pathetic offering and the others, he is obviously not fit to do the job in the first place.

Des MacHale

My name is an anagram of toilets.

T. S. Eliot

Fat people are brilliant in bed. If I'm sitting on top of you, who's going to argue?

Jo Brand

In the course of the book *250 Times I Saw a Play*, the author fails to mention what the play was, who wrote it, where it was performed and who acted in it.

Brian Lake

An author's first duty is to let down his country.

Brendan Behan

Now Barabbas was a publisher.

Thomas Campbell

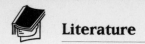 **Literature**

I was sent an author's questionnaire to help Norwegian sales. Under "Hobbies?" I listed "Tattooing snakes on sailors' bottoms".

Evelyn Waugh

The ideal reader of my novels is a lapsed Catholic and a failed musician, short-sighted, colour-blind, auditorily biased, who has read the same books that I have read.

Anthony Burgess

It's no fun having dinner with other writers. They have crap social skills, poor personal hygiene and toxic jealousy.

Celia Brayfield

I have known her pass the whole evening without mentioning a single book, in fact anything unpleasant at all.

Henry Reed

Publishers' offices are now crammed with homosexuals who have a horror of any writing with balls in it.

Marshall McLuhan

William Wordsworth keeps one eye on a daffodil and the other on a canal share.

Walter Savage Landor

With sixty staring me in the face, I have developed inflammation of the sentence structure and a definite hardening of the paragraphs.

James Thurber

If only I had taken up golf earlier and devoted my whole time to it instead of writing stories and things, I might have my handicap down to under eighteen.

P.G. Wodehouse

Your Majesty, do not hang George Wither lest it be said that I am the worst poet in the kingdom.

John Denham

The more I read Socrates, the less I wonder they poisoned him.

Thomas B. Macaulay

Watership Down: frankly I would prefer to read a novel about civil servants written by a rabbit.

Craig Brown

In the case of poets, the most important thing for them to do is to write as little as possible.

T.S. Eliot

Carlyle finally compressed his *Gospel of Silence* into thirty handsome octavo volumes.

Lord Morley

Always read stuff that will make you look good if you die in the middle of it.

P.J. O'Rourke

Literature

If a young writer can refrain from writing, he shouldn't
hesitate to do so.

André Gide

A magnum opus is a book which when dropped from a
three-storey building will kill a man.

Edward Wilson

An English novel is a story in which two people fall in love
and then complain to each other for four hundred pages.

Colin Bowles

Living — Family and Relations

If you want the world to beat a path to your door, just try to take a nap on a Saturday afternoon.

Sam Ewing

The years between fifty and seventy are the hardest. You are always asked to do things and yet you are not decrepit enough to turn them down.

T.S. Eliot

I've been forty and I've been fifty and I can tell you forty is better.

Cher

In high school my acne was so bad, blind people tried to read my face.

Joan Rivers

We stayed at the Royal Marin Hotel where we collapsed into bed only to be eaten alive by mosquitoes which could break a child's leg with a kick.

W.C. Fields

Any resemblance between Chico and Harpo and living persons is purely coincidental.

Groucho Marx

Never play peekaboo with a child on a long plane trip. There's no end to the game. Finally you have to grab him by the bib, and shout, "Look it's always going to be me!"

Rita Rudner

I never met a kid I liked.

W.C. Fields

Where are you dying tonight?

Evelyn Waugh

I have so many skeletons in the cupboard I can hardly shut
the door.

Alan Clark

The proof that we don't understand death is that we give
dead people a pillow.

Jerry Seinfeld

I take my children everywhere, but they always find their
way back home again.

Robert Orben

My father was quite eccentric: he once told staff not to
accept faxes from India because there was a plague outbreak
there.

Antonia Owen

I never go to bed because so many people die there.

Mark Twain

The only two things that middle-aged men do with greater
frequency are urinate and attend funerals.

Fred Shoenberg

The baby is wonderful: it has a bridge to its nose which the nurse says is a proof of genius! It also has a superb voice, which it freely exercises: its style is essentially Wagnerian.

Oscar Wilde

You can take it as understood, that your luck changes only if it's good.

Ogden Nash

It never amazes me that a baby can be born unable to see, hear, speak, walk or even solve *The Sun's* coffee-time crossword, but is capable of generating a sound so loud it can dislodge masonry at forty paces.

Jeremy Clarkson

There are three ages of man: youth, middle age and "You're looking terrific".

Fulton J. Sheen

This time of year fills me with sadness. It was ten years ago today that I lost my wife. I'll never forget that poker game.

Henny Youngman

If Einstein and Shaw couldn't beat death, what chance have I got?

Mel Brooks

Having one child makes you a parent; having two makes you a referee.

David Frost

If you have money, spend it. First on necessities such as drink, and then if there is anything left over, on food, shelter and clothing.

Stephen Behan

Nowadays, two can live as cheaply as one large family used to.

Joey Adams

You kids are disgusting, skulking around here all day, reeking of popcorn and lollipops.

W.C. Fields

When my wife is away and I am left to keep house for myself, I know it is time to do the washing–up when I put something on the kitchen table and something falls off the other end.

John D. Sheridan

I knew I was an unwanted baby when I saw my bath toys were a toaster and a radio.

Joan Rivers

A good place to meet a man is at the dry cleaners. These men usually have jobs and bathe.

Rita Rudner

The natural term of the affection of the human animal for its offspring is six years.

George Bernard Shaw

Not everybody hates me: only the people who've met me.
Emo Philips

I think women deserve to have more than twelve years between the ages of twenty-eight and forty.
James Thurber

Bachelorhood, like being alive, is more depressing than anything but the known alternative.
P. J. O'Rourke

If a man's character is to be abused, say what you will, there's nothing like a relation to do the business.
William Makepeace Thackeray

I pick the loser every time. If ever you see me in a queue at the railway booking office, join the other one; because there'll be a chap at the front of mine who is trying to send a rhinoceros to Tokyo.
Basil Boothroyd

It sometimes happens, even in the best families, that a baby is born. This is not necessarily a cause for alarm. The important thing is to keep your wits about you and borrow some money.
Elinor Smith

I am often asked which of us Gabor girls is the eldest. Actually, it's Mama, but she would never admit it.
Zsa Zsa Gabor

When I was born, I was so surprised I couldn't talk for a year and a half.

Gracie Allen

I'm in pretty good shape for the shape I'm in.

Mickey Rooney

The greatest advantage of not having children must be that you can go on believing that you are a nice person. Once you have children, you realise how wars start.

Fay Weldon

Husbands are a small band of men, armed only with wallets, besieged by a horde of wives and children.

P. J. O'Rourke

Hawaii: it's got everything. Sand for the children, sun for the wife and sharks for the mother-in-law.

Ken Dodd

All I desire for my own burial is not to be buried alive.

Lord Chesterfield

John Adams was a man of great, if intermittent, magnanimity.

Denis Brogan

My son has taken up meditation. At least it's better than sitting and doing nothing.

Max Kauffman

Living — Family and Relations

I cannot see why there is all this fuss about the human race being perhaps wiped out in the near future. It certainly deserves to be.

Philip Larkin

My husband and I have discovered a foolproof method of birth control. An hour with the kids before bedtime.

Roseanne Barr

I grew up with six brothers. That's how I learned to dance: waiting for the bathroom.

Bob Hope

The only time a bachelor's bed is made is when it is in the factory.

P. J. O'Rourke

I read one psychologist's theory that said "Never strike a child in anger". When should I strike him? When he is kissing me on my birthday?

Erma Bombeck

Nobody ever knew exactly how much Cordie Mae weighed but her daddy used to say, "If I could get $1.25 a pound for that child, I could pay off my truck."

Lewis Grizzard

They told me that as I got older, I would get wiser. At that rate I should be a genius by now.

George Burns

It is true that I was born in 1962. And the room next to it was 1963.

Joan Rivers

You know you are getting old when everything hurts. And what doesn't hurt, doesn't work.

Hy Gardner

A woman knows all about her children. She knows about dental appointments and football games and romances and best friends and favourite foods and secret fears and hopes and dreams. A man is vaguely aware of some short people living in the house.

Dave Barry

Babies are too vulgar for me. I cannot bring myself to touch them.

H.L. Mencken

Inside every seventy-year-old is a thirty-five-year-old asking, "What happened?"

Ann Landers

The parents complained that the youngsters never wrote but Grandma said she'd sent a letter and got a reply within days. She received a pleasant page of happy chatter, ending with, "And Grandma, you did mention that you were enclosing a cheque, but there was none in the letter."

Gene Perrett

"You will not find your father greatly changed," remarked Lady Moping, as the car turned into the gates of the County Asylum.

Evelyn Waugh

A woman just had her fourteenth child and ran out of names: to call her husband.

Milton Berle

Birth was the death of him.

Samuel Beckett

Practically anything you say will seem amusing if you're on all fours.

P. J. O'Rourke

The trouble about being retired is that you never get a break from it.

Tom Farmer

Meal time is the only time in the day when children resolutely refuse to eat.

Fran Lebowitz

My uncle was a great man, he told me so himself. "I am a great man," he said, and you cannot argue with facts like that.

Spike Milligan

The great secret in life is not to open your letters for a fortnight. At the expiration of that period you will find that nearly all of them have answered themselves.

Arthur Binstead

Early one June morning in 1872 I murdered my father: an act which made a deep impression on me at the time.

Ambrose Bierce

Key to the door: eighteen, twenty-one or five if both parents are working.

Mike Barfield

Personally I have nothing against work, particularly when performed quietly and unobtrusively by someone else.

Barbara Ehrenreich

As far as I know, a single man has never vacuumed behind a couch.

Rita Rudner

My wife and I traipsed along to natural childbirth classes, breathing and timing. We were a terrific team and had a swell time. The actual delivery was slightly more difficult. I don't want to name names, but I held my end up.

Dave Barry

I was in show business when the Dead Sea wasn't even sick.

George Burns

Big-money national lottery winners have been found statistically to be no happier than those paralysed following a major car accident, six months after each event.

Raj Persaud

Think about it. You're lying paralysed, have been for six months, but you think, ah well, it could be worse, I could have won the lottery.

Hunter Davies

I don't know if he is dead or not, but they took the liberty of burying him.

James Joyce

The best thing to do is to behave in a manner befitting one's age. If you are sixteen or under, try not to go bald.

Woody Allen

Having dinner with my mother-in-law was quite an experience: watching her pick the cabbage out of her teeth with her Iron Cross.

Les Dawson

It's really posh in the area I've moved to. Dog muck's in real neat piles and no rent-men's eyelashes hanging out of the letterboxes.

Bobby Thompson

Of all forty-two alternatives, running away is best.

Will Rogers

Living — Family and Relations

All happiness depends on a leisurely breakfast.

John Gunther

I am the oldest living man, especially at seven in the morning.

Robert Benchley

I hate the word housewife; I don't like the word home-maker either. I want to be called "domestic goddess".

Roseanne Barr

When a man has a birthday he takes a day off. When a woman has a birthday, she may take as much as five years off.

E. C. McKenzie

If you have never seen a total eclipse just watch the groom at a wedding.

Herbert V. Prochnow

If God had to give a woman wrinkles, he might at least have put them on the soles of the feet.

Ninon de Lenclos

Ask not for whom the bell tolls: let the answering machine get it.

Jean Kerr

I have my eighty-seventh birthday coming up soon and people ask me what I'd most appreciate getting. I'll tell you: a paternity suit.

George Burns

Living — Family and Relations

True maturity is reached only when a man realises he has become a father figure to his girlfriends' boyfriends: and he accepts it.

Larry McMurty

A solved problem creates two new problems and the best prescription for happy living is not to solve any more problems than you have to.

Russell Baker

I admire a housewife who can stand there and watch her husband pack his own lunch in the morning.

Brenda Davidson

Having a baby is like suddenly getting the world's worst roommate, like having Janis Joplin with a bad hangover and P.M.S. come to stay with you.

Anne Lamott

I have found little good about human beings. In my experience most of them, on the whole, are trash.

Sigmund Freud

When in doubt, use brute force.

Ken Thompson

Although prepared for martyrdom, I was willing to have it postponed.

Winston Churchill

Living — Family and Relations

It is an unwritten law that teenagers must dress alike to assert their independence.

Joyce Armor

Am I happy? What do you take me for, an idiot?

Charles De Gaulle

I told my mother-in-law that my house was her house and she said, "Get the hell off my property."

Joan Rivers

When your furnace explodes you call in a so-called professional to fix it. The "professional" arrives in a truck with lettering on the sides and deposits a large quantity of tools and two assistants who spend the better part of the week in your basement whacking objects at random with heavy wrenches, after which the "professional" returns and gives you a bill for slightly more money than it would cost you to run a successful campaign for the U.S. Senate.

Dave Barry

What do I dislike about death? Perhaps it's the hours.

Woody Allen

Nothing you can't spell will ever work.

Will Rogers

May your troubles in the coming New Year be as short-lived as your resolutions.

E. C. McKenzie

When you get married, the man becomes the head of the house. And the woman becomes the neck, and she turns the head any way she wants to.

Yakov Smirnoff

A man who goes into a supermarket for a few items would rather walk around the market balancing them than put them in one of those little baskets.

Rita Rudner

If Mr. Vincent Price were to be co-starred with Miss Bette Davis in a story by Mr. Edgar Allen Poe directed by Mr. Roger Corman, it could not fully express the pent-up violence and depravity of a single day in the life of the average family.

Quentin Crisp

A sweater is a garment worn by a child when its mother is feeling chilly.

Ambrose Bierce

Everyone who has ever walked barefoot into his child's room late at night hates Lego.

Tony Kornheiser

My father left when I was quite young. Well actually, he was asked to leave.

George Carlin

Notoriously insensitive to subtle shifts in mood, children will persist in discussing the colour of a recently sighted cement mixer long after one's own interest in the topic has waned.

Fran Lebowitz

My father won his great gamble with the future. He died.

Quentin Crisp

If you stay in a house and you go to the bathroom and there is no toilet paper, you can always slide down the banisters. Don't tell me you haven't done it.

Paul Merton

The truly enchanting thing about small children is that they don't insist on showing you photographs of their grandparents.

Niall Toibin

One cat in a house is a sign of loneliness, two of barrenness and three of sodomy.

Edward Dahlberg

I believe John Gotti wears $2,000 suits. I didn't know it was possible to buy one so cheaply.

Alan Clark

Peter O'Toole looks as if he's walking around just to save on funeral expenses.

John Huston

Living — Family and Relations

The wolf will never come to my door. He knows I'd drag him in and eat him.

Brendan Behan

When I am trying to manage the kids at Christmas I can understand why some animals eat their young.

Brendan O'Carroll

Excuse me, I didn't recognise you. I've changed so much.

Oscar Wilde

Father's Day is like Mother's Day, except the gift is cheaper.

Gerald F. Lieberman

The sins of the father are often visited upon the sons-in-law.

Joan Kiser

There is no such thing as a tough child. If you boil them first for seven hours, they all come out tender.

W.C. Fields

When a kid asks an experienced father how much a certain building weighs, he doesn't hesitate for a second. "Three thousand, four hundred and fifty-seven tons," he says.

Dave Barry

"You should see what a fine-looking man he was before he had all those children," the Arapesh tribesman told me.

Margaret Mead

Living — Family and Relations

My mother hated me. She once took me to an orphanage and told me to mingle.

Phyllis Diller

The sexual briefing that I got from my father was memorable for the way that it avoided textbook jargon and came directly to the point. He told me I was never to use a men's room in the Broadway subway. This dissertation left a certain gap in the story of procreation.

Ralph Schoenstein

Laundry increases exponentially with the number of children.

Miriam Robbins

Next to striking of fire and the discovery of the wheel, the greatest triumph of what we call civilisation was the domestication of the human male.

Max Lerner

Most men are secretly still mad at their mothers for throwing away their comic books which would be very valuable now.

Rita Rudner

At age fifty-eight I am in the prime of senility.

Joel C. Harris

McAvity accused him of canine ancestry on his mother's side.

Bob Hope

You think you'll do some little job, perfectly simple, but Fate isn't going to have it. I once sat down to put some new cotton wool in a cigarette lighter and before I'd finished I'd got all the floorboards up in the spare bedroom.

Basil Boothroyd

I haven't heard of anybody who wants to stop living on account of the cost.

Kin Hubbard

I ask people why they have deer heads on their walls and they say, "Because it's such a beautiful animal." Well I think my mother is attractive, but I have photographs of her.

Ellen DeGeneres

He was hairy. This man was not born, she thought. He was knitted by his grandmother on a cold day.

Isla Dewar

"Listen, love," I said to the wife, "you just stop at home and do the cooking and the cleaning and the washing and the ironing and the gardening and the shopping and the painting and the decorating, because I don't want my wife to work."

Johnny Carson

I hear the newspapers say I am dying. The charge is not true. I would not do such a thing at my time of life.

Mark Twain

If you think women are the weaker sex, try pulling the blankets back to your side.

Stuart Turner

Longevity is one of the more dubious rewards of virtue.

Ngaio Marsh

A kid knocked over my beer with a frisbee at the beach once. I threatened him with a lawsuit and then put this curse on him: "May your voice never change and your zits win prizes at county fairs."

Lewis Grizzard

The only advantage of old age is that you can sing while you brush your teeth.

George Burns

There is only one thing wrong with the younger generation: a lot of us don't belong to it any more.

Bernard Baruch

Native Americans give each other names which reflect their behaviour and personality. That's why I call my bloke, "Sits in Front of the Telly Farting".

Jo Brand

A parent is a person who gives a lecture on nutritional values to a youngster who has reached six foot by eating potato crisps.

Dan Looby

Living — Family and Relations

After forty a woman has to choose between losing her face or her figure. My advice is to keep your face and stay sitting down.

Barbara Cartland

The only reason my mother-in-law wasn't on Noah's ark was because they couldn't find another animal that looked like her.

Phyllis Diller

If you want to get pregnant, book the trip of a lifetime. You'll be pregnant before the tickets arrive.

Esther Selsdon

Adolescence is Nature's way of preparing parents to welcome the empty nest.

Patricia Adams

Giving away baby clothes and nursery furniture is a major cause of pregnancy.

Esther Selsdon

Hyperactivity is antisocial behaviour in one's own children, as opposed to antisocial behaviour in other people's children which simply lack parental control.

Michael O'Donnell

One trouble with growing older is that it gets progressively tougher to find a famous historical figure who didn't amount to much when he was your age.

Bill Vaughan

In a household with children, any deck of playing cards will have between thirty-eight and fifty-one cards.

Esther Selsdon

My granny lived on tinned salmon, snuff and porter, and never got out of bed except for funerals.

Brendan Behan

If you want to be adored by your peers and have standing ovations wherever you go, live to be over ninety.

George Abbott

Advanced old age is when you sit in a rocking chair and can't get it going.

Eliakim Katz

I'm beginning to understand those animals you read about where the mother has got to hide the young so the father won't eat them.

W. C. Fields

I remember the time I was kidnapped and they sent a piece of my finger to my father. He said he wanted more proof.

Rodney Dangerfield

The idea of Prince Charles conversing with vegetables is not quite so surprising when you remember that he's had plenty of practice chatting to members of his own family.

Jaci Stephens

Love, Sex, Marriage, Men and Women

Women like silent men. They think they are listening.

Marcel Achard

My girlfriend has the most beautiful breasts in the world: five.

Emo Philips

When you get married you forget about kissing other women.

Pat Boone

I can see you now, bending over a hot stove: but I can't see the stove.

Groucho Marx

I never knew any woman who could compare with Dolly Lestrange in the art of drawing out and waking into rampant life any spice of the devil which might be lurking latent in a man's soul.

Rhoda Broughton

No wonder that girl was licking David Mellor's toes. She was probably trying to get as far away from his face as possible.

Tommy Docherty

I was in San Francisco when the great earthquake struck, but we were kinda busy in the bedroom and we didn't notice what was going on outside.

John Barrymore

When a man talks dirty to a woman, it's sexual harassment.
When a woman talks dirty to a man, it's $3.95 a minute.

Steven Wright

Women will sometimes admit making a mistake. The last man
who admitted that he was wrong was General George Custer.

Rita Rudner

One of the principal differences between a woman and a
volcano is that a volcano doesn't fake eruptions.

Tim Dedopulos

Dear wife, I acknowledge receipt of your complaint number
387,501.

W. C. Fields

The morning the wife and I broke up you could hear a pin
drop in our house. I didn't see the hand grenade in her
other hand.

Roy Brown

A man who won't lie to a woman has very little
consideration for her feelings.

Olin Miller

It is only man, whose intellect is clouded by his sexual
impulses, that could give the name of "the fairer sex" to that
undersized, narrow-shouldered, broad-hipped and short-
legged race.

Arthur Schopenhauer

Bridge is not a sex substitute. Sex is a bridge substitute. The partnership is as intimate as marriage.

Helen Knott

She said she would scream for help. I told her I didn't need any help.

Bob Hope

The first man that can think up a good explanation of how he can be in love with his wife and another woman is going to win that prize they're always giving out in Sweden.

Mary Cecil

I wasn't being free with my hands: I was trying to guess her weight.

W. C. Fields

Love is being able to squeeze your lover's spots.

Zoe Ball

There is nothing wrong with pregnancy. Half of the people in the world wouldn't be here today if it wasn't for women being pregnant.

Sarah Kennedy

Whatever you say against women, they are better creatures than men, for men were made of clay, but women were made of man.

Jonathan Swift

Love, Sex, Marriage...

A man who says his wife can't take a joke forgets she took him.

John Simpson

During sex my girlfriend always wants to talk to me. Just the other night she called me from a motel.

Rodney Dangerfield

Before getting married, find out if you're really in love. Ask yourself, "Would I mind getting financially destroyed by this person?"

Johnny Carson

Two is company. Three is fifty bucks.

Joan Rivers

Be careful of men who are bald and rich; the arrogance of "rich" usually cancels out the niceness of "bald".

Rita Rudner

All men make mistakes, but married men find out about them sooner.

Red Skelton

I refuse to take a D.N.A. test to establish if I am the father of an eighteen-year-old beauty queen. I admit I have fathered at least eleven children by five different women, but this case could open the floodgates to dozens of other claims. I might run out of blood.

Joseph Estrada

Anyone who thinks that marriage is a fifty-fifty proposition doesn't understand women or fractions.

Jackie Mason

After seven years of marriage, I'm sure of just two things: first, never wallpaper together, and second, you'll need two bathrooms, both for her.

Dennis Miller

Then I said to her, "So you're a feminist: how cute."

Robin Williams

Women do laundry every couple of days. A man will wear every article of clothing he owns, including his surgical pants that were hip about eight years ago, before he will do his laundry. When he is finally out of clothes, he will wear a dirty sweatshirt inside out, rent a U-haul and take his mountain of clothes to the Laundromat, and expect to meet a beautiful woman there.

Dave Barry

Three wise men? You must be joking.

Rita Rudner

I never saw two fatter lovers, for she is as big as Murray. Seriously speaking it is a very good marriage, and acting under the direction of medical men, with perseverance and the use of a stimulating diet, there may be an heir to the house of Henderland.

Sydney Smith

One night I made love from one o'clock to five past two. It was the time they put the clocks forward.

Gary Shandling

Never marry a widow unless her first husband was hanged.

James Kelly

I am the most desirable man in the world. Indeed, if I put my mind to it, I am sure I could pass the supreme test and lure Miss Taylor away from Mr. Burton.

Noel Coward

My name is Grace but everyone calls me Gracie for short.

Gracie Allen

Marry me Emily and I'll never look at another horse.

Groucho Marx

Dior's New Look: these are clothes worn by a man who doesn't know women, never had one and dreams of being one.

Coco Chanel

Marriage is natural: like poaching, or drinking or wind in the stummick.

H.G. Wells

When a man's best friend is his dog, that dog has a problem.

Edward Abbey

She was built like a brick chickenhouse.

W. C. Fields

For their twenty-fifth wedding anniversary, they gave each other inscribed tombstones. Hers read "Here lies my wife, cold as usual" while his read "Here lies my husband, stiff at last".

Jack South

Lewis Carroll was as fond of me as he could be of anyone over the age of ten.

Ellen Terry

Personally I don't see why a man can't have a dog and a girl. But if you can afford only one of them, get a dog.

Groucho Marx

I was married by a judge but I should have asked for a jury.

Groucho Marx

Some people think my wife is pretty and others think she's ugly. Me: I think she's pretty ugly.

Les Dawson

We had a lot in common. I loved him and he loved him.

Shelley Winters

Husbands are like fires. They go out when unattended.

Zsa Zsa Gabor

The only woman I have ever loved has left me and finally married: my mother.

Emo Philips

You may marry the man of your dreams, ladies, but fourteen years later you're married to a couch that burps.

Roseanne Barr

I knew right away that Rock Hudson was gay when he did not fall in love with me.

Gina Lollobrigida

To have a happy marriage, tell your spouse everything, except the essentials.

Cynthia Nelms

Both marriage and death ought to be welcome. The one promises happiness, doubtless the other assures it.

Mark Twain

There is, of course, no reason for the existence of the male sex except that sometimes one needs help with moving the piano.

Rebecca West

Nothing in our culture, not even home computers, is more overrated than the epidermal felicity of two featherless bipeds in desperate congress.

Quentin Crisp

Marriage is an outmoded silly convention started by the cavemen and encouraged by the florists and the jewellers.

Olivia de Havilland

A girl phoned me the other day and said, "Come on over, there's nobody home." I went over. Nobody was home.

Rodney Dangerfield

Sex is something the children never discuss in the presence of their elders.

Rodney Dangerfield

Ms. is a syllable which sounds like a bumblebee breaking wind.

Hortense Calisher

It was out of the closet and into the streets for the nation's homosexuals in the 1970s. This didn't do much for the streets but, on the other hand, your average closet has improved immeasurably.

John Weidman

It takes only four men to wallpaper a house, but you have to slice them thinly.

Jo Brand

I didn't get too many women running after me. It was their husbands who'd be after me.

Charlie George

Love, Sex, Marriage...

When I was young it was considered immodest for the bride to do anything on the honeymoon except to weep gently and ask for glasses of water.

Noel Coward

Madam, if you wish to have a baby by me, surely you don't mean by unartificial insemination.

James Thurber

I have known couples stay up till three in the morning, each hoping that the other would finally give in and make the bed.

Katharine Hepburn

How many husbands have I had? You mean apart from my own?

Zsa Zsa Gabor

If you want to find out some things about yourself – and in vivid detail too - just try calling your wife fat.

P. J. O'Rourke

Stan Waltz has decided to take unto himself a wife but he hasn't decided whose yet.

Peter de Vries

Men don't shop even for their own underpants.

Germaine Greer

I don't worry about terrorism. I was married for two years.

Sam Kinison

Two cures for love: 1. Don't see him. Don't phone or write a letter. 2. The easy way: get to know him better.

Wendy Cope

Marilyn Monroe and Joe Demaggio have divorced. It just goes to show that no man can be expert at our two national pastimes.

Joe E. Brown

Men are always better at offering women things that men like: a man will give his wife a pair of fishing boots in his size.

Katharine Whitehorn

Don't you realise that as long as you have to sit down to pee, you'll never be a dominant force in the world? You'll never be a convincing technocrat or middle manager. Because people will know. She's in there sitting down.

Don DeLillo

One thing men can do better than women is read a road map. Men read maps better because only a male mind could conceive of an inch equalling a hundred miles.

Roseanne Barr

The trouble with men is that there are not enough of them.

Hermione Gingold

She was the original good time that was had by all.

Bette Davis

A sure sign a man is going to be unfaithful is if he has a penis.

Jo Brand

Sex at ninety-three is like playing snooker with a rope.

George Burns

I'm always attracted to the wrong kind of guy: like the Pope.

Carol Leifer

I read recently that love is entirely a matter of chemistry. That must be why my wife treats me like toxic waste.

David Bissonette

Whatever you may look like, marry a man of your own age: as your beauty fades, so will his eyesight.

Phyllis Diller

"Duck behind the sofa," she told me. "There's no duck behind the sofa," I told her.

Groucho Marx

We were fast and furious: I was fast and she was furious.

Max Kauffman

Is that a gun in your pocket, or are you just pleased to see me?

Mae West

Commitment is what every woman wants; men can't even spell it.

Laura Zigman

The high-heeled shoe is a marvellously contradictory item; it brings a woman to a man's height but makes sure she cannot keep up with him.

Germaine Greer

Marriage is very difficult. Very few of us are fortunate enough to marry multimillionaire girls with thirty-nine-inch busts who have undergone frontal lobotomies.

Tony Curtis

If I never see that woman again, it's too soon.

Groucho Marx

At every party there are two kinds of people: those who want to go home and those who don't. The trouble is they are usually married to each other.

Ann Landers

No two women are alike, in fact no one woman is alike.

Alfred Austin

Love, Sex, Marriage...

My wife and I were married in a toilet: it was a marriage of convenience.

Tommy Cooper

My wife and I have enjoyed over forty years of wedded blitz.

Hugh Leonard

Men get such brilliant ideas during sex because they are plugged into a genius.

Mary Lynch

How do you know if it's time to wash the dishes and clean your house? Look inside your pants. If you find a penis in there, it's not time.

Jo Brand

Fighting is essentially a masculine idea; a woman's weapon is her tongue.

Hermione Gingold

Never trust a woman who wears mauve, whatever her age may be, or a woman over thirty-five who is fond of pink ribbons. It always means they have a history.

Oscar Wilde

Marriage is a triumph of habit over hate.

Oscar Levant

I walked into that wedding with both eyes shut. Her brother shut one and her father shut the other.

Billy Bennett

I have learned that only two things are necessary to keep one's wife happy. First, let her think she's having her own way. And second, let her have it.

Lyndon Johnson

I am sorry to say that the generality of women who have excelled in wit have failed in chastity.

Elizabeth Montagu

I live by a man's code, designed to fit a man's world, yet at the same time I never forgot that a woman's first job is to choose the right shade of lipstick.

Carole Lombard

It is when your boyfriend asks you to accompany him on a river trip, at night, in the boat he has built at evening classes that a crisis comes. There is no tactful way to tell a man he has a leaky vessel.

Grace Bradbury

The word androgyny is misbegotten: conveying something like John Travolta and Farrah Fawcett-Majors Scotch-taped together.

Mary Daly

If you have been married more than ten years, being good in bed means you don't steal the covers.

Brenda Davidson

I saw on television the other day some men who like to dress up as women and when they do they can no longer parallel park.

Roseanne Barr

Do you realise that Eve was the only woman who ever took a man's side?

Milton Berle

Women do not find it difficult nowadays to behave like men, but they often find it extremely difficult to behave like gentlemen.

Compton Mackenzie

A wife can often surprise her husband on their wedding anniversary by merely mentioning it.

E.C. McKenzie

My sister gives me the creeps: all her old boyfriends.

Terri Kelly

I think the only good thing to be said about leotards is that they're a very effective deterrent against any sort of unwanted sexual attention. If you're wearing stretch knickers, and stretch tights, and a stretch Lycra leotard, you might as well try and sexually harass a trampoline.

Victoria Wood

I am tired of being a free finishing school for men.

Suzanne Wolstenholme

One special form of contact which consists of mutual approximation of the mucous membranes of the lips in a kiss has received a sexual value among the civilised nations, though the parts of the body do not belong to the sexual apparatus and merely form the entrance to the digestive tract.

Sigmund Freud

My husband and I didn't sign a pre-nuptial agreement. We signed a mutual suicide pact.

Roseanne Barr

Do we have impotent men in here tonight? Oh, I see, you can't get your arms up either.

Roseanne Barr

Woman is fickle. Give her a tickle.

Ken Dodd

Love, Sex, Marriage...

Rule One: The sun will rise in the East. Rule Two: As long as there are rich men trying not to feel old, there will be young girls trying not to feel poor.

Julie Burchill

If I did not wear torn pants, orthopaedic shoes, frantic dishevelled hair, that is to say, if I did not tone down my beauty, people would go mad. Married men would run amuck.

Brenda Ueland

Kathy Sue Loudermilk was a lovely child and a legend before her sixteenth birthday. She was twenty-one, however, before she knew an automobile had a front seat.

Lewis Grizzard

Women are most fascinating between the ages of thirty-five and forty, after they have won a few races and know how to pace themselves. Since few women ever pass forty, maximum fascination can continue indefinitely.

Christian Dior

Most married couples, even though they love each other very much in theory, tend to view each other in practice as large teeming flaw colonies, the result being that they get on each other's nerves and regularly erupt into vicious emotional shouting matches over such issues as toaster settings.

Dave Barry

Women have simple tastes. They can get pleasure out of the conversation of children in arms and men in love.

H.L. Mencken

I hate the sound of an ambulance. My first wife ran away with an ambulance driver and every time I hear a siren, I get the shakes thinking he might be bringing her back.

Jackie Martling

When women go wrong, men go right after them.

Mae West

Alan Clark is not sixty-five going on sixteen. He is sixty-five going on twelve.

Jane Clark

She was about six feet tall and had a bosom as shapeless as a plate of scrambled eggs.

Richard Gordon

Dolly Parton has a yacht in Seattle and it's windy there. One day she hung her bra to dry and woke up in Brazil.

Phyllis Diller

I bought my wife a sex manual but half the pages were missing. We went straight from foreplay to post-natal depression.

Bob Monkhouse

My girlfriend was so big she could breastfeed Watford.

Brian Conley

Most husbands remember where and when they got married. What stumps them is why.

E. C. McKenzie

Before we got married, my wife was my secretary, now she's my treasurer.

Bob Goddard

In olden times, sacrifices were made at the altar, a custom which is still continued.

Helen Rowland

If you want to stay single, look for the perfect woman.

Ken Alstad

She was a pretty nice guy: for a girl.

Robert Mitchum

Women don't gamble as much as men because their total instinct for gambling is satisfied by marriage.

Gloria Steinem

My girlfriend has to have a kidney transplant but I'm not worried about her because she hasn't rejected an organ for over twenty years. Seriously though, she could count all the lovers she's had on one hand: if she's holding a calculator.

Tom Cotter

If you ask your husband if he still loves you he will answer, "I'm still married to you, aren't I?"

Brenda Davidson

I got married again last year because my first wife died in a wishing well.

Tony Gerrard

When you hit seventy you sleep sounder, you feel more alive than when you were thirty. Obviously it's healthier to have women on your mind than on your knees.

Maurice Chevalier

Women have more imagination than men. They need it to tell us how wonderful we are.

Arnold Glasow

If you ask for a doggy bag on a date, you might as well wrap up your genitals too, because you're not going to be needing them for a long time.

Jerry Seinfeld

When my husband complained to me that he couldn't remember when we last had sex I said, "Well I can, and that's why we ain't doing it."

Roseanne Barr

My wife and I are inseparable. Sometimes it takes four people to pull us apart.

Milton Berle

When I lived with a homosexual photographer, it was so nice to relax with that kind of man, to enjoy his delightful malicious wit and intelligence, without having to worry about bruising his male ego, his machismo, and having to deal with all that ritualised wrestling at the end of an otherwise cheerful evening.

Katherine Anne Porter

I know so much about men because I went to night school.

Mae West

A woman seeking a husband is the most unscrupulous of all beasts of prey.

George Bernard Shaw

When a woman says she wants to go out and get a job to express herself, it usually means she is hopelessly behind in the ironing.

Oliver Reed

On some of the Pacific Islands there were so few women that the guys in the forces would start howling at the sight of two coconuts close together.

Bob Hope

Being a woman is a terribly difficult trade, since it consists principally of dealing with men.

Joseph Conrad

My ex-wife Joan Collins is a commodity who would sell her own bowel movements.

Anthony Newley

I didn't suspect it was an orgy until three days later.

S.J. Perelman

There are rumours floating around that I am a lesbian, which I assume were started by men who were really jealous that I was such a looker yet so unattainable.

Jo Brand

The difference between my wife and a terrorist is that you can negotiate with a terrorist.

Frank Carson

I met this girl is a bar who said she would do anything I wanted for a hundred dollars. So I handed over the money and said, "Paint my house."

Jackie Martling

On our honeymoon my husband told me to unbutton my pyjamas, and I wasn't wearing any.

Phyllis Diller

Anything worth doing well is worth doing slowly.

Gypsy Rose Lee

Since I've been married I don't have to worry about bad breath. I never get a chance to open my mouth.

Rodney Dangerfield

Never work for a man shorter than yourself and never break wind while making love. These are the only immutable laws in life.

Richard Girling

A faithful woman is one who doesn't want two men to suffer at the same time.

Jan Vercammer

My wife and I thought we were in love but it turned out to be benign.

Woody Allen

A toy company announced it is coming out with a brand-new virtual pet that eats, sleeps, burps and passes wind. It is designed to show young women what it's like to be married.

Conan O'Brien

The trouble with men and urinals is that men aren't demanding enough. If they hit something, they're happy.

Rita Rudner

Husbands think we should know where everything is: like the uterus is the tracking device. He asks me, "Roseanne, do we have any cheetos left?" Like he can't go over to the sofa and lift it himself.

Roseanne Barr

A caring husband is a man so interested in his wife's happiness that he will hire a detective to find out who is responsible for it.

Milton Berle

The greatest tragedy is to marry a man for love and then find out he has no money.

Zsa Zsa Gabor

Philandering with a married woman is the most exaggerated form of amusement that has ever been invented.

Somerset Maugham

When a man sends flowers it is a sign that he admired more women than one.

Somerset Maugham

Media and Films

If it wasn't for Venetian blinds it would be curtains for all of us.

Billy Wilder

In every movie scene which includes a person carrying a bag of groceries, the bag will invariably contain a long, skinny, French baguette loaf, and exactly 8.5 inches will be exposed.

Michael J. Pilling

The title "Little Napoleon" in Hollywood is equivalent to the title "Mister" in any other community.

Alva Johnson

William Mannix had a sound journalistic sense of what makes a good story, but no idea that this should relate to something that is actually happening.

Norman Moss

It was a cute picture. They used the basic story of *Wuthering Heights* and worked in the surfriders.

Neil Simon

The language in prison was worse than Channel Four.

Sheila Bowler

Imagine how your bum feels after sitting on a motorbike for twenty-four hours. Now imagine that feeling all over your body and you get a fair idea of the appeal of this Mickey Rourke biker picture.

Simon Rose

Media and Films

A party was thrown in Hollywood in 1966 for the wrap up of the Marlon Brando film *A Countess from Hong Kong*. The party was such a success and the film such a flop, it was suggested they should dump the film and release the party.

Brian Behan

The special effects in the movie are the worst ever. It doesn't help that the anti-heroine's height varies noticeably from shot to shot, rarely reaching the requisite fifty feet.

Christopher Tookey

Several tons of dynamite are set off in the movie *Tycoon*; none of it under the right people.

Jame Agee

The only good acting you see nowadays is from the losing nominees on Oscar night.

Will Rogers

An epic is any film so unnecessarily long that one has to go out and urinate during it.

Mike Barfield

If you buy your husband or boyfriend a video camera, for the first few weeks he has it, lock the door when you go to the bathroom. Most of my husband's early films end with a scream and a flush.

Rita Rudner

My father carried around the picture of the kid who came with his wallet.

Rodney Dangerfield

The writers and editors of *Coronation Street* should be extradited to Spain and put on show trial for crimes against humanity and 3,000 disappeared character actors.

A.A. Gill

The third secret of Fatima, the Coca-Cola formula and the appeal of Ally McBeal: these are the three mysteries of our time.

Martin James

What I said to them at half-time would be unprintable on the radio.

Gerry Francis

If *Confidential Magazine* continues to publish slanderous pieces about me, I shall feel compelled to cancel my subscription.

Groucho Marx

I read in the newspapers that the German army had invaded France and was fighting the French, and that the English expeditionary force had crossed the Channel. "This," I said to myself, "means war." As usual, I was right.

Stephen Leacock

I'd like to think every director I've worked with has fallen a little in love with me. I know Dorothy Arzner did.

Joan Crawford

My show is always screened after nine o'clock at night: my face frightens children.

Jay Leno

If you want to keep a secret, tell it to the BBC Press Office.

John Cleese

The best time I ever had with Joan Crawford was when I pushed her down the stairs in *Whatever Happened to Baby Jane?*

Bette Davis

In the 1930s, bosoms came back in again, so I was in luck, but Carole Lombard required some artificial help. Before she would go before the camera, she was famous for yelling out to her costumers, "Bring me my breasts."

Joan Crawford

I was led to believe that the new TV series *Sex in the City* would involve lots of intimate physical contact. I've seen more intimate physical contact on *Match of the Day*.

A.A. Gill

Darryl Zanuck is the only man in Hollywood who can eat an apple through a tennis racquet.

David Norris

I flew to London on the Concorde. It goes faster than the speed of sound, which is fun. But it's a rip-off because you couldn't hear the movie until two hours after you got there.

Howie Mandel

Michael Redgrave and Dirk Bogarde in *The Sea Shall Not Have Them*: I don't see why not, everyone else has.

Noel Coward

For John Ford, nothing was impossible: for an actor.

John Wayne

Charlie Chaplin was the greatest ballet dancer who ever lived and if I had got the chance I would have killed him with my bare hands.

W. C. Fields

If the Y2K bug does kick in and all modern machinery reverts to 1900 mode, those good ol' boys at ITV won't feel a thing.

Danny Baker

Look at movie stars, they took their skin from their ass and stuck it on their face. The skin on the ass was the last to wrinkle. They all walked around in their later years with buttock faces.

Charles Bukowski

Media and Films

I've made so many movies playing a hooker that they don't pay me in the regular way any more. They leave it on the dresser.

Shirley MacLaine

The trouble with the movie business is the dearth of bad pictures.

Samuel Goldwyn

The BBC has no business buying sports rights: it ought to be doing programmes about sparrows in Serbia and the lower-crested rhubarb hunter.

Kelvin MacKenzie

Bo Derek does not understand the concept of Roman numerals. She thought we fought in World War Eleven.

Joan Rivers

I love the weight of American Sunday newspapers. Pulling them up off the floor is good for the figure.

Noel Coward

I don't care what you say, for me or against me, but for heaven's sake, say something about me.

Nellie Melba

John McCririck looks like a hedge dragged through a man
backwards.

Clive James

She works at Paramount all day and Fox at night.

Mae West

Show business is worse than dog eat dog. It's dog doesn't
return other dog's phone call.

Woody Allen

Oscar winners under "other categories" are defined as "films
you would never pay to see, even if the only alternative was
staying home and watching Demi Moore in *Striptease*".

Joe Joseph

An actress I knew: when I filmed with her, I was thirty-one
and she was thirty-six. Today, I'm forty and she's still only
thirty-seven.

Tony Curtis

In television police films, why do they always say "Attention
all eunuchs"?

Sheila Huffman

Gerry and the Pacemakers movie *Ferry Cross the Mersey* was a
little glimpse into hell.

Kenneth Tynan

Media and Films

Kirk Douglas would be the first to tell you that he's a difficult man. I would be the second.

Burt Lancaster

Keep an eye on that time: that will give you a good indication of how fast the athletes are running.

Ron Pickering

We all steal, but if we are smart, we steal from great directors. Then we can call it influence.

Krzystof Kieslowski

What do I look for in a script? Days off.

Spencer Tracy

Snakes: why does it always have to be snakes?

Harrison Ford

Joan Crawford would have made an ideal prison matron, possibly at Buchenwald.

Harriet van Horne

What do I think of Kierkegaard? What movies was he in?

Pamela Anderson

Some of my friends said they didn't think I behaved too badly on *Wogan*. Like Alex Higgins and Oliver Reed, for example.

George Best

I'm not handsome in the classical sense. My eyes droop, the mouth is crooked, the teeth aren't straight, the voice sounds like a Mafioso pallbearer, but somehow it all works.

Sylvester Stallone

To refuse awards is another way of accepting them with more noise than is normal.

Peter Ustinov

At the end, Schwarzenegger makes his ritual preparations for the climatic showdown, decking himself out in leather, packing up an arsenal of guns, and, as he leaves his apartment, copping a quick look of satisfaction in the mirror. It's his only love scene.

Pauline Kael

In Westerns you are permitted to kiss your horse, but never your girl.

Gary Cooper

Here's a good one to try: if you're ever on TV just beside the person being interviewed, mouth, but do not say, "I hope all you ******* lip readers are enjoying this."

George Carlin

People are always dying in *The Times* who don't seem to die in other papers, and they die at greater length and maybe even with a little more grace.

James Reston

Media and Films

All television is children's television.

Richard Adler

I don't care what you say about me as long as you say
something about me, and as long as you spell my name right.

George M. Cohen

Johnny Depp puts the dire in director.

Edward Porter

The Daily Mail is written by office boys for office boys.

Lord Salisbury

Alistair Cooke had the idea for *Letter from America* so long
ago that Marconi is credited with inventing radio in order to
get the programme on the air.

Peter Bernard

There are just three certainties in life: death, taxes and
television repeats.

Neil Hassett

If the world does end, we will of course bring you full
coverage here on Radio Four. *The Archers* will continue on
long wave.

Eddie Mair

They're doing things on television these days that I wouldn't do in bed: even if I could.

Bob Hope

The fact that I did not marry George Bernard Shaw is the only real disappointment I've had.

Jean Arthur

Jack Ford's idea of a love story is Ward Bond and John Wayne.

Philip Dunne

Pure drivel tends to drive ordinary drivel off the TV screen.

Marvin Kitman

Awards are like piles, sooner or later every bum gets one.

Maureen Lipman

When they made Carrie Crowley they threw away the mould, but some of the mould clearly grew back.

Liam Fay

Harry, we've got a little prize for you, a two-week all expenses paid trip on a torpedo.

Steve Allen

I will have you remember that a Goldwyn comedy is not to be laughed at.

Samuel Goldwyn

Media and Films

Mickey Rooney's favourite exercise is climbing tall people.
Phyllis Diller

Citizen Kane? Not one good car chase in the whole movie.
Simon Rose

Twenty stone and encrusted in warts, imagine a toad
wearing a dinner jacket, that was Dennis Shaw: the face that
closed a thousand cinemas.
Jeffrey Bernard

Rambo isn't violent. I see Rambo as a philanthropist.
Sylvester Stallone

Cleopatra was the biggest asp disaster in the world.
Pauline Kael

I am amazed at radio D.J.s today. I am firmly convinced that
AM on my radio stands for Absolute Moron. I will not
begin to tell you what FM stands for.
Jasper Carrot

I have come up with a sure-fire concept for a hit television
show, which would be called *A Live Celebrity Gets Eaten by a
Shark*.
Dave Barry

Of course I know that all the pages of our paperbacks fall out in the reading. You don't think we want the damn things to last for ever, do you?

Clarence Paget

You can always tell a detective on TV. He never takes his hat off.

Raymond Chandler

Little girls who wear glasses in movies tell the truth. Little boys who wear glasses in movies always lie.

Gene Siskel

In Hollywood a marriage is a success if it outlasts milk.

Rita Rudner

Michael Jackson is known as the carrier bag: white, plastic and best kept away from kids.

Angus Deayton

All those who think Mia Farrow should go back to making movies where the devil gets her pregnant and Woody Allen should go back to dressing up as a human sperm, please raise your hands.

Dave Barry

Warren Beatty is forty above the waist and fourteen below it.

Shirley MacLaine

Media and Films

I'll tell you what sort of guy I was. If you ordered a boxcar full of sons-of-bitches and opened the door and found only me inside, you could consider your order filled.

Robert Mitchum

If Arnold Schwarzenegger hadn't existed we would have had to build him.

John Milius

The way things are going, I'd be more interested in seeing Cleopatra play the life of Elizabeth Taylor.

Earl Wilson

It is very hard for anything to make it out of Hollywood these days without a lame-ass wimpout ending tacked on at the whining request of test audiences selected from the most puerile of the Nielsen families, who are, as we know, chosen on the basis of the number of cousin-cousin marriages in their family over the last ten generations.

Nix Thompson

Marlon Brando attracts women like faeces attract flies.

Anna Kashfi

Table for Five would be an ideal movie to watch on a plane; at least they provide free sick bags.

Simon Rose

One time I went to a drive-in movie in a cab. The movie cost me $500.

Steven Wright

Raquel Welch is silicone from the knees up.

George Masters

The correct relationship between the media and politicians ought to be that between a dog and a lamppost.

H.L.Mencken

Anybody who ever worked on any picture for the Marx Brothers said he would rather be chained to a galley and lashed at ten minute intervals until the blood spurted from his frame than ever work for those sons of bitches again.

S.J. Perelman

Michael Fish and his pals make John Peel look like a man who was expelled from the Hellfire Club for bad behaviour.

A.A. Gill

Our old mistakes do come back to haunt us. Especially with video.

Peter O'Toole

In this world there are two kinds of people, my friend: those with loaded guns and those who dig. You dig.

Clint Eastwood

My most recent movie was a disaster movie. I didn't plan it that way.

Mel Brooks

What kind of director is David Lean? He's a tall director.

Robert Mitchum

I keep Radio Three on all the time, just to deter burglars.

Joan O'Hara

In movies, humans are violently killed with impunity, but dogs are never killed. Thus, an alien race studying films would conclude that dogs are gods.

Paul Cassel

My girlfriend is a movie actress. I'd love to see her in 3D. That's my hotel bedroom.

Benny Hill

Clive James walks like a man who has just discovered there is no paper.

A.A. Gill

I come from a family of seven boys, and the only thing we all had in common was that none of us ever won an Academy Award.

Bob Hope

Sam Goldwyn, Louis B. Mayer and Harry Cohn would have all sold their mothers, but Cohn would have delivered her.

Bob Hope

I would be insulted if a picture of mine didn't get an X-rating.

Mae West

After my screen test, the director clapped his hands gleefully and yelled: "She can't talk! She can't act! She's wonderful!"

Ava Gardner

After *Psycho*, a man wrote to me saying that his wife was afraid to take a bath or a shower. I suggested that he send her to be dry-cleaned.

Alfred Hitchcock

A retraction is the revision of an insult to give it wider circulation.

Ambrose Bierce

I tune into antiques programmes only to savour the expressions on the faces of the grasping old codgers who have just heard that the cobwebby pile of tat they have been hoarding under the bed for half a century is actually a cobwebby pile of tat after all and not a voucher to be cashed in for a trough of loot that could in turn be hoarded under the bed for another half a century.

Liam Fay

An associate producer is the only guy in Hollywood who will associate with a producer.

Fred Allen

There is not enough money in Hollywood to lure me into making another picture with Joan Crawford. And I like money.

Sterling Hayden

I learned right in the beginning from Jack Ford, and I learned what not to do by watching Cecil De Mille.

Howard Hawks

A *London Times* editor spent many years researching and writing a book called *A History of the Royal Mail*. Unfortunately, after all those years of dedication, his only manuscript got lost in the mail.

Ross Bergman

When I go to a movie I cannot relax unless I see a car chase and some breasts: even if it's just Thora Hird.

Jonathan Ross

I have a face that would stop a sundial.

Charles Laughton

I don't know how long a child will remain utterly static in front of the television, but my guess is that it could be well into their thirties.

A.A. Gill

No self-respecting fish would be wrapped in a Murdoch newspaper.

Mike Royko

Jeremy Paxman pulled every face in his repertoire.

Paul Hoggart

Television is an idiot's lantern.

Clement Attlee

Comment is free but facts are on expenses.

Tom Stoppard

My radio is thickly encrusted with muesli after years of breakfast time railings against injustice and pomposity.

Billy Connolly

Americans call it the *Tonight Show* so they can remember when it is on.

Jo Brand

Shirley Temple had a smile that could melt the glue out of a revolving bookcase.

S. J. Perelman

Only television can embarrass you to the point of having to stick your fingers in your ears and auto-asphyxiate yourself with the sofa.

A.A. Gill

You can trace most big stars to the crap telly period of their careers. It's always such a joy to watch something like *Bonanza* and spot someone like Sir Laurence Olivier dressed up as a barmaid spitting on the floor.

Jo Brand

Television has raised writing to a new low.

Samuel Goldwyn

I only play the Terminator; Tom Arnold married one.

Arnold Schwarzenegger

Journalism is the only thinkable alternative to working.

Jeffrey Bernard

Zsa Zsa Gabor had three or four operations on her nose and it got worse every time. It looks like an electric plug that you put in a wall.

Anita Ekberg

If someone vomits watching one of my films it's like getting a standing ovation.

John Waters

In the early days of television the best programme was called *Closedown*. It lasted most of the night.

Kevin McAleer

She asked me to film her best side but I told her I couldn't because she was sitting on it.

Alfred Hitchcock

Just when you think advertising has scraped the bottom of the barrel of indecency, they lower the bottom.

Michael Antebi

Ed Sullivan will be around as long as someone else has talent.

Fred Allen

Duckworth's editing and proof-reading is a disgrace.

Jeremy Lewis

This is the Suicide Hotline: please hold.

Ruby Wax

Medicine and Doctors

Have you ever had this tooth pulled before?

W. C. Fields

You can pick your friends and you can lead a horse to water, but you can't keep your eyes open when you sneeze.

Al Yankovic

L-I-M-P pronounced limp.

Spike Milligan

Medical care in Europe is excellent, and you may rest assured that if God forbid anything were to happen to you, the hospital personnel will use only the highest-quality stainless steel drill to bore a hole in your skull to let out the evil spirits.

Dave Barry

I haven't half put on a lot of weight: I used to be only seven pounds two ounces.

John Maloney

My husband, Mr. Merton, cannot travel. Once he gets outside of Stockport he can't call his bowels his own.

Mrs. Merton

The American Medical Association has stated that the leading cause of death among Americans returning from trips is being attacked by refrigerator mould.

Dave Barry

Medicine and Doctors

Two bats were hanging up in a cave and one said to the other, "When I'm older, I hope I don't become incontinent."

Mick Miller

He decided to commit suicide or die in the attempt.

Spike Milligan

When you get old, everything is hurting. When I get up in the morning, it sounds like I'm making popcorn.

Lawrence Taylor

The trouble with Viagra is that it can keep you stiff: permanently.

Dave Letterman

Doctor, feel my purse.

Jane Ace

How come you can always read a doctor's bill but never his prescription?

Finley Peter Dunne

The other day I got on a weighing machine that stamps out your weight on a card. When the card came out it read, "Come back in ten minutes: alone."

Jackie Gleason

How long have you had that birthmark?

W. C. Fields

I have gained and lost the same ten pounds so many times my cellulite must have déjà vu.

Jane Wagner

Tests on twenty students who thought they had fallen in love revealed a common pattern of brain cells similar to that of people suffering an obsessive-compulsive disorder.

John Follian

My biological clock is ticking so loudly I'm nearly deafened by it. They search me going into planes.

Marian Keyes

There is only one type of doctor who needs to wear a bow tie and that's a gynaecologist.

Martin Fischer

Good cheekbones are the brassière of old age.

Barbara De Portago

I've been on a diet for the last two decades. I've lost a total of 789 pounds. By all accounts I should be hanging from a charm bracelet.

Erma Bombeck

The hypothalamus controls the "four fs": fighting, fleeing, feeding and mating.

Martin Fischer

Aristotle was famous for knowing everything. He taught that the brain exists merely to cool the blood and is not involved in the process of thinking. This is true only of certain persons.

Will Cuppy

During the anatomy lesson the lecturer told us that the human male's testicles were about the size of a partridge's egg. A female student sitting next to me nudged me and said, "At least I know now how big a partridge's egg is."

Richard Gordon

Hypochondria is the imaginary complaint of indestructible old ladies.

E.B. White

On the other hand you have five fingers.

Steven Wright

I don't mind giving them a reasonable amount of blood, but a pint: why that's very nearly an armful.

Tony Hancock

If the patient isn't dead, you can always make him worse if you try hard enough.

Frank Vertosick

Once you start buying first-aid kits you start having accidents.

George Mikes

Medicine and Doctors

David Borenstein

I never go to a dentist who's had his office soundproofed.

Milton Berle

Mummy and I take so many pills, we rattle.

Raine Spencer

I have cancer: my veins are filled, once a week, with a Neapolitan carpet cleaner distilled from the Adriatic and I am as bald as an egg. However, I still get around and am mean to cats.

John Cheever

I have a left shoulder-blade that is a miracle of loveliness. People come miles to see it. My right elbow has a fascination that few can resist.

W. S. Gilbert

The most common error made in matters of appearance is the belief that one should disdain the superficial and let the true beauty of one's soul shine through. If there are places on your body where this is a possibility, you are not attractive, you are leaking.

Fran Lebowitz

Caution: living may be dangerous to your health.

Willard Espy

Medicine and Doctors

The medical profession wasn't always the highly organised racket that it is today.

Flann O'Brien

I'm fat and proud of it. If someone asks me how my diet is going, I say, "Fine, how was your lobotomy?"

Roseanne Barr

I have flabby thighs but fortunately my stomach covers them.

Joan Rivers

Every man who feels well is a sick man neglecting himself.

Jules Romains

The worst thing about a lung transplant is coughing up somebody else's phlegm.

Jackie Martling

A sure cure for toothache is to tickle a mule's heel.

Ken Alstad

My book *Venereal Disease and Its Prevention* is affectionately dedicated to my wife.

Felix Leblanc

She suffers badly from tinnitus: ringing in the ears, and they're wedding bells.

Richard Gordon

Medicine and Doctors

My husband Norm has invented a revolutionary heat-seeking bedpan.

Edna Everage

The Mayo Clinic was named after its founder, Dr. Ted Clinic.

Dave Barry

One of the most pleasing sounds of springtime to be heard all over the country is the contented cooing of osteopaths as Man picks up his garden spade.

Oliver Pritchett

Never drop dead around a specialist.

S.J. Perelman

I cannot abide the obstetrical anecdotes of ancient dames.

H.L. Mencken

Operating on the wrong patient or doing the wrong side of the body makes for a very bad day.

Frank Vertosick

I've got Parkinson's Disease. I can shake a Margarita in five seconds.

Michael J. Fox

After a certain age, if you don't wake up aching in every joint, you're probably dead.

Tommy Mein

He was a man of unbounded stomach.

William Shakespeare

Middle age is when anything new you feel is most likely a symptom.

Sidney Body

For every day you spend in hospital, you need a week to recuperate.

Esther Selsdon

I was once engaged when I was forty and I found it gave me very serious constipation. So I broke off the engagement and the lady quite understood.

Arthur Smith

When doctors in Los Angeles went on strike back in 1976, the local death rate fell by eighteen per cent.

Ross Bergman

My wife had but two topics of conversation: the Royal family and her bowels.

Alan Bennett

Tonsils and adenoids are lumps of lymphoid tissue that exist only to provide food, clothes and private education for the children of ear, nose and throat surgeons.

Michael O'Donnell

Madness takes its toll; please have exact change ready.

Steven Wright

The menopause: if I want hot flushes and depression I'll stick to aerobics.

Jo Brand

Why do women always carry bags and why are those bags so often heavy? Is the tote bag an exterior uterus, the outward sign of the unmentionable burden?

Germaine Greer

I don't consider myself bald. I'm simply taller than my hair.

Tom Sharpe

We regret to announce that Mr. Bernard Manning who was told by his doctor either to lose ten stone or die, has just lost ten stone.

Rowan Atkinson

What a disgusting verdict: he choked on his own vomit. You never hear of anyone choking on some one else's vomit.

Jeffrey Bernard

Music

God dammit! Jimmy Hendrix beat me to dying.

Janis Joplin

I must shut my ears. The man of sin rubbeth the hair of the horse to the bowels of the cat.

John O'Keeffe

I once worked in a circus beside a drum so loud that in a short time I was able to hear only disturbances like thunder, explosions and collapsing buildings.

W. C. Fields

Lloyd Webber's music is everywhere but so is AIDS.

Malcolm Williamson

There are few moments during her recital when one can relax and feel confident that she will make her goal, which is the end of the song.

Paul Hume

A new survey shows that one out of every four drivers has fallen asleep at the wheel while on the road. And for half of those the last thing they remember hearing is "And now here's a new one from John Tesh."

Dennis Miller

I prefer flying on Concorde because I cannot get in and out of aircraft toilets but on a three and a half hour flight I can hold out.

Luciano Pavarotti

The worst feature of a new child is its mother's singing.
Kin Hubbard

I know only two tunes. One of them is "Yankee Doodle".
The other isn't.
Ulysses S. Grant

Abstain from wine, women and song; mostly song.
Brad Templeton

Composers should not think too much: it interferes with
their plagiarism.
Howard Dietz

There won't be a Beatles reunion as long as John Lennon
remains dead.
George Harrison

Did you write the words or the lyrics?
Bruce Forsyth

The purpose of jazz is the destruction of music.
Thomas Beecham

Mothers used to breastfeed their babies while I played the
piano: I guess they used to find it soothing. I played the odd
very sudden loud note because I loved to watch the nipples
shooting out of their mouths.
Harpo Marx

Dudley Moore is such a clever little pianist. He can play on the white keys and the black.

Noel Coward

The Queen's distaste for dreary repetition fills me with admiration. Sent a rare invitation from the Royal Opera House to see *The Marriage of Figaro*, she politely sent her regrets because she had already seen it.

Jasper Gerard

Luciano Pavarotti is only slightly smaller than Vermont.

Norman Lebrecht

The music is in German. You would not understand it.

Oscar Wilde

Twentieth-century music is like paedophilia. No matter how persuasively and persistently its champions urge their cause, it will never be accepted by the public at large, who will continue to regard it with incomprehension, outrage and repugnance.

Kingsley Amis

The Spice Girls is a five-member girl group with the talent of one bad actress between them.

David Hutcheon

My girlfriend, she was thin. Two more navels and she would have been a flute.

Stu Francis

Men who listen to classical music tend not to spit.

Rita Rudner

People are wrong when they say that opera is not what it used to be. It is what it used to be. That is what is wrong with it.

Noel Coward

Members of the orchestra, we cannot expect you to be with us all the time, but perhaps you could be good enough to keep in touch now and again.

Thomas Beecham

He's my favourite kind of musician. He knows how to play the ukulele, but he doesn't.

Will Rogers

Dana International looked as if she had smeared herself with superglue before colliding with a flock of crows.

Paul Hoggart

Offenbach's music is wicked. It is abandoned stuff: every accent in it is a snap of the fingers in the face of moral responsibility; every ripple and sparkle on its surface twits me for my teetotalism, and mocks at the early rising of which I fully intend to make a habit some day.

George Bernard Shaw

I hate music: especially when it is played.

Jimmy Durante

Undeterred, his weekend now in ruins, the young Wolfgang answered the by now more insistent Prince Leopold's entreaties and proceeded to speedily pen his fifty-second symphony, which he finished by the following Tuesday.

Peter Bruce

My Fair Lady: I must say Bernard Shaw is greatly improved by music.

T. S. Eliot

If Rock 'n' Roll is here to stay I might commit suicide.

Sammy Davis Jr.

This is a very old English folksong. I know it is a very old English folksong because I wrote it myself when I was very young.

Paddy Roberts

A bodhran is a large, round, thick-skinned object, usually tight, which you have to hit with a stick to get anything out of. Elsewhere in the world this is known as a husband.

Terry Eagleton

If I had a hammer, I'd use it on Peter, Paul and Mary.

Howard Rosenberg

Adolf Hitler was one of the first rock stars. Look at some of his films and see how he moved. I think he was quite as good as Mick Jagger.

David Bowie

Once after Caruso had sung a duet with a celebrated soprano, more noted for her beauty than her voice, he was asked how he liked her singing. "I don't know," he replied, "I never heard her."

Dorothy Caruso

At the rehearsals I let the orchestra play as they like. At the concert I make them play as I like.

Thomas Beecham

Let's face it, we became ingrown, clannish and retarded. Cut off from the mainstream of humanity, we came to believe that pink is "flesh-colour", that mayonnaise is a nutrient and that Barry Manilow is a musician.

Barbara Ehrenreich

An "orchestra" in radio circles is any ensemble comprising more than three players, while a "symphony" programme is one that includes Liszt's Liebenstraum.

Deems Taylor

The problem with Lloyd Webber's music is not that it sounds as if it were written by other composers, but that it sounds as if it were written by Lloyd Webber.

Gerald Kaufman

Dear Mr. Edison, I am astonished at the wonderful form you have developed and terrified at the thought that so much hideous and bad music will be put on records for ever.

Arthur Sullivan

 **Music**

At Gloucestershire Airport we used to broadcast cassette
tapes with birds' distress sounds on them to keep the runway
clear of seagulls, blackbirds and rooks. They didn't work very
well so now we use Tina Turner records: the birds really hate
her, especially "Simply the Best".

Ron Johnson

Italian singing: bestial howling and entirely frantic vomiting
up of damned souls through their still carnal throats.

John Ruskin

Listen, kid, take my advice. Never hate a song that has sold
half a million copies.

Irving Berlin

I don't like my music, but what is my opinion against that of
millions of others?

Frederick Loewe

King's College Chapel: it's the building. That acoustic would
make a fart sound like a sevenfold amen.

David Willcocks

Irving Berlin had a voice that sounded like a hoarse tomcat
with its tail in a clothes wringer.

Bob Hope

I hope Harry Secombe dies before me because I don't want
him singing at my funeral.

Spike Milligan

When we couldn't get a seat in the pub, we used to play "O Superman" by Laurie Anderson on the jukebox. It worked every time.

Alan James

The best thing I can say about bagpipes is that they don't smell, too.

Brendan Behan

I wrote a song, but I can't read music. Every time I hear a new song on the radio, I think, "Hey, maybe I wrote that."

Steven Wright

A manager of a cinema in South Korea decided that the *Sound of Music* was too long to show so he edited out all the songs.

Ross Bergman

The only thing a bassoon is good for is kindling an accordion fire.

Ross Bergman

Have you heard about the fellow who played "Flight of the Bumble Bee" on the tuba? He blew his liver out.

Tommy Boyd

Stravinsky looks like a man who was potty-trained too early and his music proves it as far as I am concerned.

Russell Hoban

If the bassoon were any easier to play, the wrong people would be playing it.

Norman Herzberg

If anyone has conducted a Beethoven performance, and then doesn't have to go on an osteopath, then there's something wrong.

Simon Rattle

A flute is a variously perforated hollow stick intended for the punishment of sin.

Ambrose Bierce

Without question, the most unpopular medium of musical sound in the world is the trombone.

Thomas Beecham

My inability to sing has been a devastating blow.

Julie Andrews

Can you imagine finding out you've married a man who wanted to watch opera after Christmas dinner? You'd just have to beat him to death with your Sri Lankan rice steamer wouldn't you?

A. A. Gill

Of all the noises known to man, opera is the most expensive.

Voltaire

Nationalities and Places

Anyone found smiling after curfew on the streets of
Philadelphia was liable to get arrested. If a woman dropped
her glove on the street she was liable to be arrested and
hauled before a judge on a charge of strip-teasing.

W.C. Fields

All Englishmen talk as if they've got a bushel of plums stuck
in their throats and then after swallowing them get
constipated from the pits.

W.C. Fields

The American male does not mature until he has exhausted
all other possibilities.

Wilfred Sheed

A German film-goer was beaten to death in a Bonn cinema
by ushers because he had brought his own popcorn.

Karl Shaw

During the potato famine, how come the Irish couldn't
afford the cost of a square meal but could still afford to go to
America?

Steve Coogan

It is easy to understand why the most beautiful poems about
England were written by poets living in Italy at the time.

George Sanders

A donkey is a horse translated into Dutch.

G. C. Lichtenberg

I would love to speak Italian but I can't, so I grew underarm hair instead.

Sue Kolinsky

I gave him a Dublin uppercut – a kick in the groin.

Brendan Behan

Finding out your sister is black is fine; finding out that your sister is Welsh is another thing.

A. A. Gill

Wales is the land of song: but no music.

David Wulstan

Give me your tired, your poor, your huddled masses yearning to be free, provided they have satisfactorily filled-out forms 3584-A through 3597-Q.

Dwight McDonald

Philadelphia is the greatest cemetery in the world.

W.C. Fields

Knocking down a house in Dublin recently, the workmen found a skeleton with a medal on a ribbon around its neck. The inscription was: Irish Hide and Seek Champion 1910.

Frank Carson

On stage I often ask the audience if they would like to hear an Irish joke. If they say "yes", I tell them one: in Gaelic.

Ian McPherson

A group of innocent American tourists was taken on a tour bus through a country the members later described as "either France or Sweden", and subjected to three days of looking at old dirty buildings where it was not possible to get a cheeseburger.

Dave Barry

Chief amongst the mysteries of India is how the natives keep those little loin cloths up.

Robert Benchley

The colour slides we took of our trip to the Virgin Islands featured nearly two dozen shots of the airplane wing alone.

Dave Barry

In England, if you are a Duchess, you don't need to be well dressed: it would be thought quite eccentric.

Nancy Mitford

Imagine the Lord speaking French! Aside from a few odd words in Hebrew, I took it completely for granted that God had never spoken anything but the most dignified English.

Clarence Day

Pittsburg is Hell with the lid taken off.

James Parton

Irish weather consists of rain: lots of it. It has been known for the rain to cease, sometimes for as much as two weeks at a time. But when this happens, the Irish complain of drought, pestilence and imminent bankruptcy.

Stan Gebler Davies

There are no more thefts in New York: there's nothing left to steal.

Henny Youngman

I do not know the American gentleman. God forgive me for putting two such words together.

Charles Dickens

They should never have shared the Nobel Peace Prize between two people from Northern Ireland. They will only fight over it.

Graham Norton

The Welsh are such good singers because they have no locks on their bathroom doors.

Harry Secombe

The sex urge in Ireland is either sublimated by religion, dissipated in sport or drowned in drink, or in the case of Paddy Kavanagh, all three.

Niall Toibin

The population of England is thirty million, mostly fools.

Thomas Carlyle

The French are tremendous snobs, despite that rather showy and ostentatious Revolution.

Arthur Marshall

Belgium is just a country invented by the British to annoy the French.

Charles De Gaulle

I do not know the location of the Virgin Islands but at least I know that they are on the other side of the world from Maidenhead.

Winston Churchill

You have to know a man awfully well in Canada to know his surname.

John Buchan

The trouble with America is that there are far too many wide open spaces surrounded by teeth.

Charles Luckman

The Greeks: dirty and impoverished descendants of a bunch of la-de-da fruit salads who invented democracy and then forgot to use it while walking around like girls.

P. J. O'Rourke

The archives of the Turkish Foreign Office were kept in saddlebags: so much more convenient if you have to move quickly.

G. M. Young

To many, no doubt, he will seem blatant and bumptious, but we prefer to regard him as simply British.

Oscar Wilde

The real people of Ireland are the people who have their dinner in the middle of the day.

Jackie Healy-Rae

It should have been written into the armistice treaty that the Germans would be required to lay down their accordions along with their arms.

Bill Bryson

Ivan was coming with us only as far as Minsk where he was attending a village idiots' conference. The banners read "Welcome Idiots".

Woody Allen

England is the only country in the world where the food is more dangerous than the sex.

Jackie Mason

The Italians' technological contribution to mankind stopped with the pizza oven.

Bill Bryson

A naturally free, familiar, good-natured, precipitate, Irish manner had been schooled and schooled late in life into a sober, cold, stiff, deportment, which she mistook for English.

Maria Edgeworth

To learn English you must begin by thrusting the jaw forward, almost clenching the teeth, and practically immobilising the lips. In this way the English produce the series of unpleasant little mews of which their language consists.

Jose Ortega y Gasset

Brighton Pavilion looks as if St. Paul's had come down and littered.

Sydney Smith

They say the situation in Northern Ireland is not as bad as they say it is.

Denis Taylor

My French stinks. It seems that when I asked somebody for a light I asked them to set me on fire.

Jeffrey Bernard

There are only three things against living in Britain: the place, the climate and the people.

Jimmy Edwards

England will fight to the last American.

Will Rogers

The Welsh are a nation of male voice choir lovers whose only hobbies are rugby and romantic involvement with sheep.

Lenny Henry

In the game there were at least five instances of people being grabbed by the testicles. Neath is the bag-snatching capital of Wales.

Dylan Thomas

I think it possible that all Scots are illegitimate, Scotsmen being so mean and Scotswomen so generous.

Edwin Muir

During World War Two, Ireland was neutral on the Allied side.

John A. Murphy

Had Cain been a Scot, God would have changed his doom.
Not forced him to wander, but confined him home.

John Cleveland

The Vicar of St. Ives says that the smell of fish there is sometimes so terrific as to stop the church clock.

Francis Kilvert

"Down there", is a polite phrase used by schoolgirls who learn it from nuns. Do not confuse it with Australia which is called "Down under".

Sterling Johnson

In the world of the British nanny there are three sorts of sin: little sins, bigger sins and taking off your shoes without undoing the laces.

Jonathan Gathorne-Hardy

Liverpool is at the moment the centre of the consciousness of the human universe.

Allen Ginsberg

The actual Irish weather report is really a recording made in 1922, which no one has had occasion to change. "Scattered showers, periods of sunshine."

Wilfrid Sheed

It is difficult to describe Norwegian charisma precisely because it is somewhere between a Presbyterian minister and a tree.

Johnny Carson

A French screwdriver is a hammer.

Reinhold Aman

I am an Englishman. I was born in Ireland: but if a racehorse is born in a pigsty, that does not make him a pig.

Arthur Wellesley

The British must be gluttons for satire: even the weather forecast seemed to be some kind of spoof, predicting every possible combination of weather for the next twenty-four hours without actually committing itself to anything.

David Lodge

The English think that incompetence is the same thing as sincerity.

Quentin Crisp

I've been under a lot of pressure recently because I originally came from the Moon.

Boothby Graffoe

Scotland is renowned for its peace and solitude. In fact, crowds from all over the world flock here to enjoy the solitude.

Stuart Collinson

I said, "It is most extraordinary weather for this time of year!" He replied, "Ah, it isn't this time of year at all."

Oliver St. John Gogarty

Rome reminds me of a man who lives by exhibiting to travellers his grandmother's corpse.

James Joyce

By midday the heat is so unbearable that the streets are empty except for thousands of Englishmen taking mad dogs for walks.

Spike Milligan

It was not until I went back to Ireland as a tourist, that I perceived the charm of my country was quite independent of the accident of my having been born in it.

George Bernard Shaw

There are so many ways to die here.

Denis Leary

Addis Ababa looks as if it has been dragged piecemeal from an aeroplane carrying rubbish.

John Gunther

It is disconcerting to be naked in a Japanese bath and to be massaged by a young girl who has picked up a few English phrases, and remarks as she is walking up and down your spine, "Changeable weather we are having lately."

Peter Ustinov

China is a big country, inhabited by many Chinese.

Charles de Gaulle

German is a most extravagantly ugly language: it sounds like someone using a sick bag on a 747.

Willie Rushton

House names are cabalistic phrases carved on pieces of wood that the English middle class place in obscure corners of their property to ward off GPs seeking them by torchlight on rainy nights.

Michael O'Donnell

New York City is the most exciting place in the world. Nothing could discredit capitalism more than a decision of the Russians to try it.

Jack Tanner

New York is the only city in the world where you can get deliberately run over on the sidewalk by a pedestrian.

Russell Baker

Nationalities and Places

I don't like Norway at all. The sun never sets, the bar never opens and the whole country smells of kippers.

Evelyn Waugh

I asked him, "Are you a pole vaulter?" He said, "No, I'm a German and how did you know my name was Walter?"

Billy Connolly

Signor Angeli, Professor of Italian at Trinity College, Dublin, was asked to translate the proceedings of the opening of Queen's College Cork into Italian and forward them to the Pope. He reported the fact that the ceremony was attended by both men and women as "There were present men of both sexes" which led a cardinal to observe that Cork must be a very queer city.

Robert Kane

For a marriage to be valid in Scotland it is absolutely necessary that it should be consummated in the presence of two policemen.

Samuel Butler

America is the only country in the world where a housewife hires a woman to do her cleaning so she can do volunteer work at the day-care centre where the cleaning woman leaves her child.

Milton Berle

If you hear anyone saying "Begorrah" during your stay in Ireland, you can be sure he's an undercover agent for the Irish Tourist Board pandering to your false expectations.

Terry Eagleton

Nationalities and Places

The French hate anything that is ugly. If they see an animal that is ugly, they immediately eat it.

Jeremy Clarkson

It's easy enough to get to Ireland. It's just a straight walk across the Irish Sea as far as I'm concerned.

Brian Clough

When it is three o'clock in New York, it's still 1938 in London.

Bette Midler

Washington, D.C. is a little too small to be a state, but too large to be an asylum for the mentally deranged.

Anne Burford

If the French were really intelligent they would speak English.

Wilfred Sheed

"Du ye think the Almighty would be understanin' siccan gibberish?" said the old Scotch lady, when, during the Napoleonic war, she was reminded that maybe a French mother was praying as fervently for victory as she was herself.

F.A. Steel

Foreigners may pretend otherwise but if English is spoken loudly enough, anyone can understand it, the British included.

P.J. O'Rourke

Where else in the world but Australia is a generous man defined as one who would give you his arsehole and shit through his ribs?

Germaine Greer

Europe is a place teeming with ill-intentioned persons.

Margaret Thatcher

In the Soviet Union there is no mystical or obscure treatment of love, such as decadent Western poets use. We sing of how a young man falls in love with a girl because of her industrial output.

Stephan Petroviv

Nobody knows what the original people of Scotland were: cold is probably the best informed guess, and wet.

A.A. Gill

I genuinely believe that one of the reasons Britain is such a steady and gracious place is the calming influence of the football results and shipping forecasts.

Bill Bryson

In Mexico a bachelor is a man who cannot play the guitar.

Lillian Day

Every time I see a picture of those people in Somalia it brings a tear to my eye. I mean I'd love to be that thin but not with all those flies and everything.

Mariah Carey

Belief in progress is a doctrine of idlers and Belgians.

Charles Baudelaire

I am inconsolable at the death of King Hussein of Jordan. I was a very good friend of Jordan: he was the greatest basketball player this country has ever seen or will see again.

Mariah Carey

In a hotel in County Mayo I saw a notice displayed over the barometer: Don't hit me. I am doing my best.

M.F. Watson

Ireland is a modern nation but it is modernised only recently and at the moment it is behaving rather like a lavatory attendant who has just won the lottery.

Terry Eagleton

I took one look at Madame Chiang Kai-Shek and thought to myself "Holy Smoke, I forgot to collect my laundry."

Jack Warner

Those who survived the San Francisco earthquake said, "Thank God, I'm still alive." But of course those who died, their lives will never be the same again.

Barbara Boxer

It's a scientific fact that if you live in California you lose one point of your I.Q. every year.

Truman Capote

Nationalities and Places

I wrote to a Tyrolean landlord in search of accommodation and received the following reply : "Do not distress yourself that I am poor in bath; I am excellent in bed."

Gerard Hoffnung

The Welsh are not meant to go out in the sun. They start to photosynthesise.

Rhys Ifans

Have you heard about the Irishman who had a leg transplant? His welly rejected it.

Frank Carson

I plan to buy the Millennium Dome, turn it upside down, float it out into the Mediterranean and rename it the Wok of Gibraltar.

Brian Conley

American is a country that doesn't know where it is going but is determined to set a speed record getting there.

Laurence J. Peter

Ask any man what nationality he would prefer to be and ninety-nine out of a hundred will tell you that they would prefer to be Englishmen.

Cecil Rhodes

When President Reagan came to Ireland, he was greeted with a beautifully ambiguous banner which read "Welcome to the Ould Sod".

Dominic Cleary

A Boston man is the east wind made flesh.

Thomas Appleton

It is an odd thing, but everyone who disappears is said to be seen in San Francisco. It must be a delightful city, and possess all the attractions of the next world.

Oscar Wilde

England is not ruined because sinewy brown men from a distant colony sometimes hit a ball further and oftener than we do.

J.B. Priestley

Hell is much like London, a populous and a smoky city.

Percy B. Shelley

Men have walked on the Sea of Tranquillity, but are still barred from walking through certain parts of Ulster.

Declan Lynch

The Japanese idea of fun is to lock a naked man in a room for eighteen months and allow him to exist only on food that he wins in competitions.

Emma Colverd

Rain is one thing the British do better than anybody else.

Marilyn French

France is the thriftiest of all nations; to a Frenchman sex provides the most economical way to have fun.

Anita Loos

A Canadian is somebody who knows how to make love in a canoe.

Pierre Berton

Awkward ministers can find themselves out in the cold: or worse still, sent off to sort out Northern Ireland.

Terrance Dicks

Help a London child: kill a social worker.

Alexei Sayle

The British Army always fights uphill, in the rain, at the junction of two maps.

Brian Horrocks

You know it is summer in Ireland when the rain gets warmer.

Hal Roach

Anyone like Ernest Hemingway who marries three girls from St. Louis hasn't learned much.

Gertrude Stein

Had Jerusalem been built in England and the site of the
Crucifixion discovered, it would promptly be built over and
called the Golgotha Centre.

Alan Bennett

In New York, tip the taxicab driver forty dollars if he does
not mention his haemorrhoids.

Dave Barry

The only way to improve Pittsburgh would be to abandon
it.

Frank Lloyd Wright

It is always a mistake trying to speak French to the Frogs. As
Noel Coward once remarked when he was sustaining a role
at the Comèdie Française, "They don't understand their own
language."

Robert Morley

The Irish equivalent of "gilding the lily" can be translated as
"rubbing lard on a sow's arse".

Niall Toibin

Dublin's O'Connell Street contains statues of Daniel
O'Connell, Charles Stewart Parnell and Lord Nelson: three
of history's best-known adulterers.

W. B. Yeats

What Switzerland lacks is manure.

André Gide

Nationalities and Places

As the Irish philosopher said, isn't one man as good as another, and a great deal better.

William Makepeace Thackeray

In the desert you don't ask anyone where they are going with a spade.

Harry Andrews

There are two modes of transport in Los Angeles: car and ambulance. Visitors who wish to remain inconspicuous are advised to choose the latter.

Fran Lebowitz

Rumour has it that the Aran Islands are rolled up when the tourist season ends and towed into Galway, where workmen chip away at the rocks to make them look a bit more rugged.

Terry Eagleton

It is possible to eat English piecrust, whatever you may think at first. The English eat it, and when they stand up and walk away, they are hardly bent over at all.

Margaret Halsey

A Glaswegian atheist is a bloke who goes to a Rangers–Celtic match to watch the football.

Sandy Strang

The English have undertaken the weighty responsibility of being the missionaries of civilisation to the world.

George Hegel

Be careful with that sword. If you kill me you have killed a sixth of the world's Welsh actors.

Richard Burton

The architectural style of Dublin's O'Connell Street is neon-classical.

Terry Eagleton

Finland, a nation of drunken Captain Birds Eyes, and Ireland, the *Big Issue* seller of Europe.

A.A. Gill

I learned a lot from my tour of South America. You'd be surprised. They're all individual countries.

Ronald Reagan

London is a large village on the Thames where the principal industries carried on are music halls and the confidence trick.

Dan Leno

He was driving at sixty-five miles an hour, which in Miami is the speed limit normally observed inside car washes.

Dave Barry

My parents didn't want to move to Florida, but they turned sixty, and it was the law.

Jerry Seinfeld

There is a fog in the Channel. The Continent is completely cut off.

Russell Brockbank

Sweden is where they commit suicide and the king rides a bicycle.

Alan Bennett

The United States has much to offer the Third World War.

Ronald Reagan

Roseanne is American and by the rules of comedy each continent is allowed only one fat female comedian. (Dawn French is in a different category from me as she is a double act.)

Jo Brand

Australians would prefer a sick dingo as president than a president elected by politicians.

Les Patterson

I saw a sign in a French restaurant: Special Today: no snails.

Gerard Hoffnung

New York is an exciting town where something is happening all the time, most of it unsolved.

Johnny Carson

Owing to the acute stresses of the work, most comics' bowels function less efficiently than the English end of the Channel tunnel.

Jo Brand

I'm going to Berlin. I'm going to personally shoot that paper-hanging son of a bitch.

George Patton

The ingredients of an authentic peasant dish will cripple any budget outside its country of origin.

Esther Selsdon

In California, handicapped parking is for women who are frigid.

Joan Rivers

Toronto will be a fine town, when it's finished.

Brendan Behan

I was born in Cardiff but at the age of six months I was persuaded by my parents to leave Wales.

Griff Rhys-Jones

One of my ministers found half-naked with a guardsman in Hyde Park? Last Wednesday? The coldest night of the year? Makes you proud to be British.

Winston Churchill

Politics

 **Politics**

A group of politicians deciding to ditch the President because his morals are bad is like the Mafia getting together to bump off the Godfather for not going to church on Sunday.

Russell Baker

The authorities were at their wits' end, nor had it taken them long to get there.

Desmond McCarthy

Congress is so strange. A man gets up to speak and says nothing. Nobody listens. Then everybody disagrees with him.

Will Rogers

It is hard to argue with the government. Remember, they run the Bureau of Alcohol, Tobacco and Firearms, so they must know a thing or two about satisfying women.

Scott Adams

I think it is absolutely tantamount.

Edward McCarthy

Margaret Thatcher even dresses to the right.

Patrick Murray

You can fool some of the people all of the time, and you can fool all of the people some of the time, but you can't fool some of the people some of the time.

Stan Laurel

Even Napoleon had his Watergate.

Danny Ozark

The Conservative Establishment has always treated women as nannies, grannies and fannies.

Teresa Gorman

I tried to tell the French Prime Minister in French that I admired the various positions he had taken on so many matters. What I actually said was that I desired the French Prime Minister in many different positions.

Tony Blair

Tony Blair is just Bill Clinton's toyboy.

Saddam Hussein

Clinton has kept all of the promises that he intended to keep.

George Stephanopolous

Campaigning for governor, there have been a couple of times when I yearned for the serenity I knew as a Marine Corps tank commander in Korea.

Adlai Stevenson

Ask not what you can do for your country, ask what your country can do for you.

Teddy Kennedy

I think it's about time we voted for senators with breasts. We've been voting for boobs long enough.

Claire Sargent

If the Lord's Prayer was introduced in Congress, Senators would propose a large number of amendments to it.

Henry Wilson

Politics is the art of preventing people from taking part in affairs that properly concern them.

Paul Valèry

It is exciting to have a real crisis like the Falklands on your hands, when you have spent half your political life dealing with humdrum issues like the environment.

Margaret Thatcher

Michael Foot is a kind of walking obituary for the Labour Party.

Chris Patten

The Lord Privy Seal is neither a lord, a privy or a seal.

Sydney D. Bailey

Politicians are people who, when they see light at the end of the tunnel, go out and buy some more tunnel.

John Quinton

The House of Lords is a body of five hundred men chosen at random from amongst the unemployed.

David Lloyd-George

An official denial is a de facto confirmation.

John Kifner

Nothing beats Reaganomics: though herpes runs it close.

Art Buchwald

The F.B.I. is filled with Fordham graduates keeping tabs on Harvard men in the State Department.

Daniel P. Moynihan

Even Al Gore has won an award and he has less star quality than head lice.

Joe Joseph

These people like Ben Elton suddenly criticising New Labour. It's the first ever recorded case of rats leaving a floating ship.

Alexei Sayle

John Prescott has been to Hull and back.

Roland Watson

The Reformed Parliament: I never saw so many shocking bad hats in my life.

Arthur Wellesley

I don't mind how much my ministers talk: as long as they do what I say.

Margaret Thatcher

The Treasury in 1850 kept a half-wit to make a nominal field against the official candidates. On one occasion he was successful.

G. M. Young

There is nothing in Socialism that a little age or a little money will not cure.

Will Durant

David Lloyd-George is a goat-footed bard, a half-human visitor to our age from the hag-ridden magic and enchanted woods of Celtic antiquity.

John Maynard Keynes

You won the elections. But I won the count.

Anastasio Somoza

Malcolm Fraser looks like an Easter Island statue with an arse full of razor blades.

Paul Keating

Bill Clinton cannot seriously oppose the gun lobby because it is part of the phallocentric culture which he has done so much to promote.

Patrick Murray

There is a simple and practical method of putting this long-suffering government out of its misery. Since sex scandals seem to be the only method of dislodging a politician from his post, it is the duty of every patriotic woman to bear a love child by a Tory M.P.

Margarette Driscoll

Government is like a baby: a huge appetite at one end and no sense of responsibility at the other.

Ronald Reagan

My wife has a very major cause and a very major interest that is a very complex and consuming issue with her. And that's me.

Dan Quayle

Never underestimate the hypocrisy of politicians.

James Herbert

There are few ironclad rules of diplomacy but to one there is an exception. When an official reports that talks were useful, it can safely be concluded that nothing was accomplished.

J.K. Galbraith

Seventy-six would not be an old age to leave office. Andrew Jackson left the White House at the age of seventy-five and he was still quite vigorous. I know because he told me.

Ronald Reagan

As a politician my only known vice is chocolate.

Carlo Ciampi

She is the lady of the mansion, she is the wife of a peer of the realm, the daughter of a marquis, has five Christian names; and hardly ever speaks to a commoner except for political purposes.

Thomas Hardy

My first qualification for the great job of being mayor of New York is my monumental personal ingratitude.

Fiorello la Guardia

The really neat thing about Dan Quayle, as you realise from the first moment you look into those lovely blue eyes, is impeachment insurance.

Barbara Ehrenreich

John Adams was a man of great, if intermittent, magnanimity.

Denis Brogan

Robin Cook's misfortune is to sound as if his voice never broke but his behaviour encourages this view.

Jacob Rees-Mogg

Democracy is the art of running the circus from the monkey cage.

H.L.Mencken

A good politician is quite as unthinkable as an honest burglar.

H. L. Mencken

Politics

I couldn't possibly vote Conservative while William Hague still leads the party. There is nothing personal in this, it's purely on class grounds.

Auberon Waugh

Vote for insanity, you know it makes sense.

Lord Sutch

The time has come for all good men to rise above principles.

Huey Long

Words cannot express my regret at the news that Anthony Wedgewood Benn has decided to retire from parliament. My regret is that he has left it twenty years too late.

Gerald Kaufman

Kings are not born; they are made by artificial hallucination.

George Bernard Shaw

The Left does not have a monopoly on ecology. We at the National Front respect life and love animals. I myself have a white rat whom I kiss every day on the mouth.

Jean-Marie le Pen

I have tried all sorts of excitement, from tip cat to tiger shooting, all degrees of gambling from beggar-my-neighbour to Monte Carlo, but have found no gambling like politics, and no excitement like a big division in the House of Commons.

Randolph Churchill

Anything any politician did with a woman other than his wife prior to May 5th 1987 ought to be allowed to go unrevealed.

Gary Hart

No country which has cricket as one of its national games has yet gone Communist.

Woodrow Wyatt

I never became a politician because I could not stand the strain of being right all the time.

Peter Ustinov

All of these black people are screwing up my democracy.

Ian Smith

The Berlin Wall was the defining achievement of Socialism.

George Will

There should have been a last line of defence during the war. It would have been made up entirely of the more officious breed of cricket stewards. If Hitler had tried to invade these shores he would have been met by a short stout man in a white coat who would have said, "I don't care who you are, you're not coming in here unless you are a member."

Ray East

The American Communist Party was notoriously infiltrated by informers. It used to be said that spies practically kept the Party going with their dues and contributions.

Helen Lawrenson

Terry Dicks is living proof that a pig's bladder on a stick can be elected as a member of parliament.

Tony Brooks

Democracy is the recurrent suspicion that more than half the people are right more than half of the time.

E. B. White

In this world of sin and sorrow, there is always something to be thankful for; as for me, I rejoice that I am not a Republican.

H. L. Mencken

Experts are saying that President Bush's goal now is to politically humiliate Saddam Hussein. Why not just make him the next Democratic presidential nominee?

Jay Leno

Roosevelt proved a man could be President for life; Truman proved anybody could be President; and Eisenhower proved you don't need to have a President.

Kenneth Keating

When they call the roll in the Senate, the Senators do not know whether to answer "Present" or "Not guilty".

Theodore Roosevelt

I never called Richard Nixon a son of a bitch; after all, he claims to be a self-made man.

Harry S. Truman

Politics

Politics has always been the systematic organisation of hatreds.

Henry Adams

Politics: a strife of interests masquerading as a contest of principles.

Ambrose Bierce

Support your local politician: with a rope.

Steve Jackson

Whatever happens will be for the worse, and therefore it is in our interest that as little as possible should happen.

Lord Salisbury

Margaret Thatcher adds the diplomacy of Alf Garnett to the economics of Arthur Daley.

Denis Healey

Edwina Curry is the female Margaret Thatcher.

Mrs. Merton

People must not do things for fun. We are not here for fun. There is no reference to fun in any Act of Parliament.

A. P. Herbert

I have had more women by accident than JFK had on purpose.

Lyndon B. Johnson

Hereditary peers sit independently, weigh arguments independently, think independently. Then they independently vote Conservative.

Lord Richards

Party Political Conferences are gatherings of the walking undead.

John Green

A politician is a statesman who approaches every question with an open mouth.

Adlai Stevenson

The difference between golf and government is that in golf you can't improve your lie.

George Deukmejian

Anthony Eden is the original banana man: yellow outside and a softer yellow inside.

Reginald Paget

The policies of the Monster Raving Loony Party include putting crocodiles in the Thames, jogging machines to make electricity for pensioners, banning January and February to make winter shorter, and the introduction of a Scottish Olympics to include caber-tossing and haggis-lifting.

Lord Sutch

If you want to succeed in politics, you must keep your conscience well under control.

Frank McNally

Politics

A leopard never changes his stripes.

Al Gore

Coolidge was the first president to discover what the American people want is to be left alone.

Will Rogers

A woman could never be President. A candidate must be thirty-five or over: and where are you going to find a woman who will admit she's over thirty-five?

E. W. Howe

The only man who ever went to Parliament with a sensible policy was Guy Fawkes.

Terrance Dicks

Someday our grandchildren will look up at us and say, "Where were you, Grandma, and what were you doing when you first realised that President Reagan was not playing with a full deck?"

Barbara Ehrenreich

George Washington never told a lie. I don't know how he ever made it in politics.

Bob Hope

The trend toward democracy is inevitable: but it can be stopped.

Dan Quayle

It is inexcusable that President Clinton was using the phone in the Oval Office for phone sex. The phone in the Oval Office is specifically for fund raising.

Dave Letterman

The business of the Civil Service is the orderly management of decline.

William Armstrong

Eisenhower will make a fine president. He was the best clerk who ever served under me.

Douglas MacArthur

Stanley Baldwin was an epileptic corpse.

Winston Churchill

Robin Cook is the only Foreign Secretary in 700 years who has more trouble at home than he has abroad. But don't mock. One day his looks will go.

John Major

When I go into the voting booth, do I vote for the person who is the best President or the slime bucket who will make my life as a cartoonist wonderful?

Mike Peters

Edmund Burke was known as "The Dinner Bell of the House of Commons". As soon as he rose to his feet, the majority of M.P.s decided it was time to take some refreshment in the Members' Dining Room.

Greg Knight

Politics

The U.S. presidency is a Tudor monarchy plus phones.
Anthony Burgess

Lloyd George spend his whole life plastering together the true and the false and therefrom manufacturing the plausible.
Stanley Baldwin

If you sneak out the back door of your girlfriend's house, it's called a Hart bypass.
Bob Hope

Now that Bobby has been assassinated, Teddy must run for the Presidency.
Rose Kennedy

You know a politician is well hung if you can't get a finger between his Adam's apple and the rope.
Dave Southwell

Michael Heseltine canvassed like a child molester hanging around the lavatories.
Norman Lamont

What do you call a Tory candidate whose name begins with "A"? The accused.
Gordon Brown

Lyndon Johnson is a man of his most recent word.
William F. Buckley

President Reagan thinks arms control means some kind of deodorant.

Patricia Schroeder

Jimmy Carter as president is like Truman Capote marrying Dolly Parton. The job is too big for him.

Rich Little

Stupidity got us here: it can get us out.

Will Rogers

Elections are just things that are held to see if the polls were right.

Joey Adams

The I.R.A. will stick to their guns on decommissioning.

Gerry Adams

Ross Perot was never a candidate, just a wake-up call with ears.

Anna Quinlan

Religion

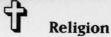

We owe a lot to the Y.M.C.A: the invention of the triangular trouser button for example.

Spike Milligan

This is not mentioned by the Synoptists, and is passed over by St. John: but full details may be found in Farrar's Life of Christ.

Geoffrey Madan

Confirmation at Eton was like a huge garden party, faintly overshadowed by a sense of religion.

A. C. Benson

I'm going to marry a Jewish woman because I like the idea of getting up on a Sunday morning and going to the deli.

Michael J. Fox

The Church of England is the best church to live in but the Catholic Church is the best church to die in.

Oscar Wilde

The bishop had forty bedrooms in his palace, but only thirty-nine articles to put in them.

Winston Churchill

There is one passage in the Scripture to which all the potentates of Europe seem to have given their unanimous assent and approbation: "There went out a decree in the days of Caesar Augustus that all the world should be taxed."

Charles Colton

Religion

Never invoke the gods unless you really want them to appear. It annoys them very much.

G. K. Chesterton

A couple of Sundays ago I was watching *Songs of Praise* on television, which was coming from Maidstone Prison of all places, when I spotted to my amazement a man who owes me fifty pounds. He was standing there and had the gall to be singing "Abide With Me".

Jeffrey Bernard

It is ungentlemanly to include more than one foreign coin in contributions to the church collection.

George Moor

It is as hard for a rich man to enter the kingdom of Heaven as it is for a poor man to get out of Purgatory.

Finley Peter Dunne

From time to time I like to pay tribute to my four scriptwriters, Matthew, Mark, Luke and John.

Fulton J. Sheen

Sin is a dangerous toy in the hands of the virtuous. It should be left to the congenitally sinful, who know when to play with it and when to let it alone.

H. L. Mencken

My religion is that I'm an alcoholic.

Brendan Behan

✝ Religion

By 1879 there was little left of religion in Ruskin except an adolescent horror of fornication.

G. M. Young

The organs of human utterance are too frail to describe my lack of interest in papal affairs.

George Lyttelton

Since we have to speak well of the dead, let's knock them while they're still alive.

John Sloan

Like most Irish people, I was born a Catholic. This came as a big shock to my parents, who were Jewish.

Michael Redmond

About a year ago, I disturbed a burglar. I said, "There is no God."

Paul Merton

First I turned one cheek, then the other cheek. Now that the scriptures have been fulfilled, I intend to beat the hell out of thee.

William Penn

She had once been a Catholic, but discovering that priests were infinitely more attentive when she was in process of losing or regaining faith in Mother Church, she maintained an enchantingly wavering attitude.

F. Scott Fitzgerald

Religion

The followers of Ian Paisley threw a rosary and a Bible at me, which I felt was at least an ecumenical gesture.

Lord Soper

Charity creates a multitude of sins.

Oscar Wilde

It is far easier to forgive an enemy after you've got even with him.

Olin Miller

The only thing that stops God sending a second flood is that the first one was useless.

Sébastien Roch Nicolas Chamfort

Punch is very much like the Church of England. It is doctrinally inexplicable but it goes on.

Malcolm Muggeridge

We know that we must return good for evil: but that may just be a mistake in translation.

John Vanbrugh

What is my opinion of the hereafter? One world at a time.

Henry Thoreau

I know I ought not to yield to temptation, but somebody must or the thing becomes ridiculous.

Anthony Hawkins

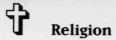

Religion

Catholics claim to be infallible, Anglicans to be always right.

Richard Steele

Zangwill's teeth are like the Ten Commandments: all broken.

Herbert Beerbohm Tree

If English was good enough for Jesus Christ, it's good enough for me.

David Edwards

Men don't get cellulite. God might just be a man.

Rita Rudner

I believe everything the Catholic Church teaches is true but I let my wife go to mass for me.

Brendan Behan

What do you say to God when He sneezes?

Steven Wright

By virtue we merely mean the avoidance of the vices that do not attract us.

Robert Lynd

I love my neighbour as myself, and to avoid coveting my neighbour's wife, I desire to be coveted by her: which you know is another thing.

William Congreve

God must love airline fares. He made so many of them.

Milton Berle

Heaven doesn't want me and Hell is scared I am going to take over.

Elizabeth Taylor

I was the child who always got picked to play Bethlehem in the school nativity play. And even then Mary and Joseph used to keep mistaking me for Greater Manchester.

Jo Brand

I always say beauty is only sin deep.

H.H.Munro

Old-fashioned vicar (Tractarian) seeks colleague; fine church; good musical tradition. Parish residential and farming. Good golf handicap an asset but not essential. Left-handed fast bowler preferred.

David Hopps

Many people believe they are attracted by God, or by Nature, when they are only repelled by man.

W.R. Inge

They used to have religious texts on the walls of the condemned cell in Durham. One of them read, "Today is the tomorrow you worried about yesterday." It was the last thing a bloke saw as he went out to be hanged.

Brendan Behan

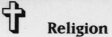# Religion

Little is known about St. Valentine except that he was born in a wood and his twin brother was carried off by a bear. Hence the tradition, begun by greeting-card moguls in the fifteenth century, of the rest of us sending expensive unsigned messages to each other.

Mel Smith

Fundamentalists are to Christianity what painting by numbers is to art.

Robin Tyler

Puritanism is no religion for a gentleman and Anglicanism is no religion for a Christian.

G.K. Chesterton

People talk of their seats in Heaven with as much confidence as if they had booked them at the box office.

Leigh Hunt

I am determined my children shall be brought up in their father's religion, if they can find out what it is.

Charles Lamb

The only thing I would not wish on my worst enemy is eternal life.

Quentin Crisp

There are terrible temptations that it requires strength, strength and courage to yield to.

Oscar Wilde

Religion

The most important things to a Southern girl are God, family, and hair, almost never in that order.

Lucinda Ebersole

I knew an eighty-five-year-old man who married a girl of eighteen. He needed someone to answer the Rosary for him.

Eamon Kelly

If you are sufficiently irascible, God might just decide to wait.

Godfrey Just

It rains only straight down. God doesn't do windows.

Steven Wright

Poor Chesterton, his day is past
Now God will know the truth at last.

E. V. Lucas

A cult becomes a religion when it progresses from killing its members to killing non-members.

David Lewin

There are no atheists on turbulent airplanes.

Erica Jong

A clever theft was praiseworthy among the Spartans; and it is equally so among Christians, provided it be on a sufficiently large scale.

Herbert Spencer

I'm a very religious person, it's just that I don't believe in God.

Eric Idle

I was one of the few brides who ever got a request from the congregation to keep the veil on.

Phyllis Diller

Religion is the fashionable substitute for belief.

Oscar Wilde

The law of headstones: the more unctuous the inscription, the more unscrupulous the rogue who lies beneath.

Michael O'Donnell

Conscience is the quiet voice that warns you not to leave any fingerprints.

Alberto Sordi

It was the afternoon of my eighty-first birthday and I was in bed with my catamite when Ali announced that the archbishop had come to see me.

Anthony Burgess

Science and Technology

I think animal testing is a terrible idea. They get all nervous and give the wrong answers.

Hugh Laurie

I am always on the lookout to replace my current computer when it becomes obsolete: usually before I get it all the way out of the box.

Dave Barry

The most difficult book I have ever read was a manual on the use of iron mangles by A. J. Thompson.

Spike Milligan

Ladies and gentlemen: the world's greatest novelty: the twins Redwood and Brentwood. Redwood is the smallest giant in the world, while his brother Brentwood is the tallest midget in the world. They baffle science.

W. C. Fields

If it wasn't for burnt toast, entire species of birds in Britain would disappear.

Jeremy Noakes

Not all chemicals are bad. Without chemicals such as hydrogen and oxygen, for example, there would be no way to make water, a vital ingredient in beer.

Dave Barry

A computer lets you make more mistakes faster than any invention in human history: with the possible exceptions of handguns and tequila.

Mitch Ratliffe

If the effort that went in research on the female bosom had gone into our space program, we would now be running hot-dog stands on the moon.

Robert Murphy

The sooner all the animals are extinct, the sooner we'll find where they've hidden their money.

Mikael Pawlo

The surest sign that intelligent life exists elsewhere in the Universe is that it has never tried to contact us.

Bill Watterson

The inside diameter of all pipes must not exceed the outside diameter, otherwise the hole will be on the outside.

Michael Stillwell

Baldrick, you wouldn't recognise a cunning plan if it painted itself purple and danced naked on top of a harpsichord singing, "Cunning plans are here again."

Rowan Atkinson

Have you ever noticed that when you blow in a dog's face he gets mad, but when you take him out in a car, he sticks his head out the window?

Steve Bluestein

I offer the modest proposal that our Universe is simply one of those things which happen from time to time.

Edward Tyron

Science and Technology

Okay: what's the speed of dark?

Wright Stevens

The Universe is a big place, perhaps the biggest.

Kilgore Trout

It's a good thing there's gravity or else when birds died, they'd stay where they were.

Steven Wright

Tell a man that there are three hundred billion stars in the Universe and he'll believe you. Tell him a bench has wet paint on it and he'll have to touch it to be sure.

Ed Jarger

Perennials are the ones that grow like weeds, biennials are the ones that die this year instead of next and hardy annuals are the ones that never come up at all.

Katharine Whitehorn

They will never really crack down on air pollution until it begins to interfere with television reception.

Francis Capelini

I know a man who has a device for converting solar energy into food. He's been doing it for years: it's called a farm.

David Stenhouse

I can only assume that God wanted penicillin and that was His reason for creating Alexander Fleming.

Alexander Fleming

Science and Technology

My dog is glad to see me every minute of my life. I come home, he jumps around. I go in the closet, I come out, he jumps around and wags his tail. I turn my face away, I turn it back, he wags his tail. Either he loves me passionately or he has absolutely no short-term memory.

Harry Weston

They say the dog is man's best friend. I don't believe that. How many of your friends have you had neutered?

Larry Reels

I don't know why they keep complaining about this greenhouse effect. If they know what's causing the problem, why don't they just stop giving people permission to build them?

Joe Lavin

Most earthquakes are caused by sudden movements of Roseanne Barr.

Joan Rivers

Programming today is a race between software engineers striving to build bigger and better idiot-proof programs and the Universe trying to produce bigger and better idiots. So far the Universe is winning.

Rich Cook

The computer world has a language all of its own, just like Hungary. The difference is, if you hang around Hungarians long enough, you start to understand what they're talking about.

Dave Barry

Science and Technology

Why don't sheep shrink when it rains?

Steven Wright

Orang-utans teach us that looks are not everything: but darned near it.

Will Cuppy

My Maltese dog Sugar is the sole reason why I stay away from Britain. You have this absurd quarantine law which no one can explain to me. Sugar is the best-behaved and most intelligent dog in the world. If she could come here she would probably be able to explain it to all of us.

Elizabeth Taylor

Bats have no bankers and they do not drink and cannot be arrested and pay no tax and, in general, bats have it made.

John Berryman

Animals generally return the love you lavish on them by a swift bite in passing: not unlike friends and wives.

Gerald Durrell

Experiments with laboratory rats have shown that, if one psychologist in the room laughs at something a rat does, all of the other psychologists in the room will laugh equally.

Garrison Keillor

The Internet is a boon: to the single man.

Frank Skinner

Science and Technology

Nitro-glycerine was invented by a French chemist in 1847 as a cure for headaches.

L. Moholy

Isaac Newton was very much smaller than a hippopotamus, but we do not on that account value him less.

Bertrand Russell

If we aren't supposed to eat animals, why are they made of meat?

Jo Brand

Never clean your C.D. with a blowtorch as it will void the warranty.

Steven Daniletto

The trouble with questions on probability is that there is not the slightest probability of any two people arriving at the same answer.

Darragh Martin

He had read Shakespeare and found him weak in chemistry.

H.G. Wells

My wife puts on a dozen creams and oils at night: elbow oil, shoulder oil, neck oil, face cream, eyelid cream, crow's-foot oil. If she caught fire, the guys who quenched the Kuwaiti wells couldn't cap her.

Milton Berle

Whenever a man comes up with a better mousetrap, nature immediately comes up with a better mouse.

James Carswell

With regards to midges, the only sensible thing to do is to rub brown sugar over all exposed areas of the body. It doesn't stop them biting, but it rots their teeth.

Iain MacLeod

We can work it out: defiant phrase used with respect to:
1. Rocky relationships
2. Video recorder operation.

Mike Barfield

The doctor has invented an extraordinary weapon which will make war less brutal. It is described as a very powerful liquid which rots braces at a distance of a mile.

J. B. Morton

The major difference between a thing that might go wrong and a thing that cannot possibly go wrong is that when a thing that cannot possibly go wrong goes wrong it usually turns out to be impossible to get at and repair.

Douglas Adams

A disabled toilet? What's the matter with it: can't it flush?

Peter O'Toole

Science and Technology

Consumers should bring their broken electronic devices to destruction centres where trained personnel would whack them (the devices) with sledgehammers. Consumers would then be free to go out and buy devices, rather than having to fritter away years of their lives trying to have the old ones repaired at so-called "factory service centres" which in fact consist of two men named Lester poking at the insides of broken electronic devices with cheap cigars and going, "Lookit all them WIRES in there."

Dave Barry

In certain cheap stores you can buy screwdrivers which break when exposed to sunlight.

Dave Barry

An experiment may be considered a success if no more than half your data must be discarded to obtain correspondence with your theory.

Brendan Connell

If people think Nature is their friend, then they sure don't need an enemy.

Kurt Vonnegut

There are two major products that come out of Berkeley: L.S.D. and U.N.I.X. We do not believe this to be mere coincidence.

Jeremy Anderson

They laughed at Christopher Columbus, they laughed at Einstein and they laughed at the Wright brothers. But they also laughed at Bozo the Clown.

Carl Sagan

Science and Technology

"User" is the computer professionals' word for an idiot.

Dave Barry

The future, according to some scientists, will be exactly like the past, only far more expensive.

John Sladek

Numbers written on restaurant bills within the confines of restaurants do not follow the same mathematical laws as numbers written on any other pieces of paper in any other parts of the Universe.

Douglas Adams

A conservation area is a place where you can't build a garage but you can build a motorway.

James Gladstone

Science is the best way of satisfying the curiosity of individuals at government expense.

L. A. Artsimovich

Spiders who have been flushed down the plug hole climb up again and stare at you through the overflow while you are sitting in the bath.

Jenni Hall

Modern science was conceived largely as an answer to the servant problem.

Fran Lebowitz

Science and Technology

A probability is a number between zero and one about which nothing else is known.

Victor Spasek

Captain Scott's party was unlucky enough to find itself on its way to the South Pole during an unusually cold snap.

Nigel Hawkes

A flashlight provides excellent storage for dead batteries.

Milton Berle

The motto of my garage seems to be: if it ain't broke, we'll break it.

Dave Barry

We've sent a man to the moon and that's a quarter of a million miles away. The centre of the earth is only four thousand miles away. You could drive that in a week but for some reason nobody's ever done it.

Andy Rooney

A mobile phone is a thin line between conspicuous success and standing in the street talking to yourself like a madman.

Mike Barfield

It is time for the human race to join the solar system.

Dan Quayle

Technology has brought meaning to the lives of many technicians.

Ed Bluestone

Science and Technology

Here is the weather forecast: it will be cool in Poole, dry in Rye and if you're living in Lissingdown, do bring an umbrella.

Ronnie Barker

Social Behaviour and
Manners

Social Behaviour and Manners

The nineteenth-century Shah of Persia never quite got the hang of English high-society etiquette. On one state visit he was introduced to the Marchioness of Londonderry: and made an offer to buy her.

Graham Nown

It is conduct unbecoming to a lady or gentleman when being treated at the V.D. clinic to name as contacts those who spurned your advances.

George Moor

Even the best-intentioned of great men need a few scoundrels around them; there are some things you cannot ask an honest man to do.

La Bruyère

A man usually has no idea what is being said about him. The entire town may be slandering him, but if he has no friends he will never hear of it.

Honoré de Balzac

Do unto the other fellow the way he'd like to do unto you, but do it first.

Edward Westcott

She has a charming fresh colour, when it is fresh put on.
Richard Brinsley Sheridan

Mass murderers are simply people who have had enough.
Quentin Crisp

It was embarrassing. I felt like a figure skater who had forgotten to put on her knickers.

Hugh Leonard

I hate to spread rumours: but what else can one do with them?

Amanda Lear

As universal a practice as lying is, and as easy as it seems, I do not remember to have heard three good lies in any conversation, even from those who were most celebrated in that faculty.

Jonathan Swift

The ruffian pretended to mistake me for a commissionaire outside the theatre and said, "Would you call me a cab?" I replied, "Yes, but not a hansom one."

James Agate

On those summer evenings a radio playing loudly can be a great source of annoyance to your neighbours. Another good way to annoy them is to set fire to their dustbins.

Marty Feldman

My motto is "My rights or I bite."

Clarinda Breujere

I stuck up for her. Someone said she wasn't fit to live with pigs and I said she was.

Brendan Behan

Duty is what one expects from others, it is not what one does oneself.

Oscar Wilde

The only thing that sustains one through life is the consciousness of the immense inferiority of everybody else and this is a feeling I have always cultivated.

Oscar Wilde

The "t" is silent, as in Harlow.

Margot Asquith

He was so mean that if he owned the Alps, he wouldn't give you a slide.

Brendan Behan

If one hides one's talent under a bushel, one must be careful to point out the exact bushel under which it is hidden.

H. H. Munro

When you ascend the hill of prosperity, may you not meet a friend.

Mark Twain

If you bed people of below-stairs class, they will go to the papers.

Jane Clark

Social Behaviour and Manners

There is nothing so annoying as to have two people go right on talking when you're interrupting.

Mark Twain

"Yes, but not in the South", with slight adjustments will do for any argument about any place, if not about any person.

Stephen Potter

Do you suppose I could buy back my introduction to you?

Groucho Marx

That poor man. He's completely unspoiled by failure.

Noel Coward

Lord Glasgow, having flung a waiter through the window of his club, brusquely ordered, "Put him on the bill."

Guy Phillips

A Merry Christmas to all my friends except two.

W. C. Fields

What a lovely hat! But if I may make one teensy suggestion? If it blows off, don't chase it.

Miss Piggy

Hats divide generally into three classes. Offensive hats, defensive hats and shrapnel.

Katharine Whitehorn

I am loath to interrupt the rapture of mourning for Queen Victoria in which the nation is now enjoying its favourite festive: a funeral: but in a country like ours the total suspension of common sense and sincere human feeling for a whole fortnight is an impossibility.

George Bernard Shaw

Before you criticise someone, you should walk a mile in their shoes. That way when you criticise them, you're a mile away and you have their shoes.

Jack Handey

All decent people live beyond their incomes nowadays, and those who aren't respectable live beyond other people's. A few gifted individuals manage to do both.

H. H. Munro

His smile explained everything; he always carried it with him as a leper carried his bell; it was a perpetual warning that he was not to be trusted.

Graham Greene

Dress simply. If you wear a dinner jacket, don't wear anything else on it: like lunch or dinner.

George Burns

The hatchet is buried but a bit of its handle may still be seen protruding from the ground.

Rhoda Broughton

Social Behaviour and Manners

It is always painful to part from people whom one has known for a very brief space of time. The absence of old friends one can endure with equanimity.

Oscar Wilde

The advantage of doing one's praising for oneself is that one can lay it on so thick and exactly in the right places.

Samuel Butler

Talk to a man about himself and he will listen for hours.

Benjamin Disraeli

If you are foolish enough to be contented, don't show it, but grumble with the rest.

Jerome K. Jerome

Yes, I am exactly like the characters in my books. I am very tough and have been known to break a Vienna roll with my bare hands. I am very handsome, have a powerful physique and change my shirt every Monday.

Raymond Chandler

I have stopped swearing. I now just say Zsa Zsa Gabor!

Noel Coward

Somebody must listen and I like to do all the talking myself. It saves time and prevents arguments.

Oscar Wilde

The bride usually has one friend who wanted to marry the groom. This girl should be maid of honour so the bride can rub it in.

P. J. O'Rourke

I belong to the most exclusive club in London. I am a friend of Randolph Churchill.

Bernard Levin

One should never make one's debut with a scandal. One should reserve that to give an interest to one's old age.

Oscar Wilde

She was a great prude, having but two lovers at a time.

Mary Montagu

Christopher Martin-Jenkins and Neil Durden-Smith were standing next to the bar, playing with each other's hyphens.

Peter Tinniswood

The depressing thing about an Englishman's traditional love of animals is the dishonesty thereof: get a barbed hook into the upper lip of a salmon, drag him endlessly around the water until he loses his strength, pull him to the bank, hit him on the head with a stone, and you may well become fisherman of the year. Shoot the salmon and you'll never be asked again.

Clement Freud

Social Behaviour and Manners

Eccentricity, to be socially acceptable, still has to have at least four or five generations of inbreeding behind it.

Osbert Lancaster

I must go home and do that which no one else can do for me.

Jonathan Swift

Dean Westcott's letter of condolence to Charles Kingsley on a bereavement: fourteen pages; only one phrase could be deciphered, apparently "ungrateful devil".

Geoffrey Madan

I expect to pass through this world but once and therefore if there is anybody that I want to kick in the crotch I had better kick them in the crotch now, for I do not expect to pass this way again.

Maurice Bowra

His aunt was a bit of a social climber, although very much on the lower slopes. I was once on a tram with her going past the gas works in Wellington Road and she said, "Alan, this is one of the biggest gas works in England. And I know the manager."

Alan Bennett

Few of us can stand prosperity. Another man's I mean.

Mark Twain

When I want your opinion I'll give it to you.

Laurence J. Peter

I could never be buried with people to whom I had not
been introduced.

Norman Parkinson

Memorial services are the cocktail parties of the geriatric set.

Harold Macmillan

The club to which I belonged displayed a notice: Will
gentlemen please refrain from using the handbasin as a
convenience during the asparagus season.

Peter Ustinov

Man is certainly a benevolent animal. A never sees B in
distress without thinking C ought to relieve him directly.

Sydney Smith

Guns don't kill people: I do.

Emo Philips

I argue very well. Ask any of my remaining friends. I can
win an argument on any topic against any opponent. People
know this, and steer clear of me at parties. Often, as a sign of
their great respect, they don't even invite me.

Dave Barry

If you want to become the perfect guest, then try to make
your host feel at home.

W.A. Nance

Social Behaviour and Manners

You lie to only two people in your life: your girlfriend and a policeman. To everyone else you tell the truth.

Jack Nicholson

Nothing more rapidly inclines a person to go into a monastery than reading a book on etiquette. There are so many trivial ways in which is it possible to commit some social sin.

Quentin Crisp

Never explain: your friends do not need it and your enemies will not believe you anyway.

Elbert Hubbard

He was so self-obsessed that he didn't notice anyone else. Even on the local nudist beach he admired only himself.

Simon Hughes

T. E. Lawrence is always backing into the limelight.

Lord Berners

I know that's a secret for it's whispered everywhere.

William Congreve

We have the highest authority for believing that the meek shall inherit the earth; though I have never found any particular corroboration of this aphorism in the records of Somerset House.

F. E. Smith

Many thanks for your note. May I recommend a good taxidermist?

Aubrey Forshaw

I met a man who told me he hadn't seen me for four years. "Quite a nice little interval, don't you think?" I replied before passing on.

Lytton Strachey

A cardinal rule is never to sit interesting people with bores. Put all the bores at one table: they don't know that they are bores and they will all have a wonderful time.

Joyce Haber

Some people mistake fun for being sectioned under the Mental Health Act.

Paul Merton

Something happens to a man when he puts on a necktie. It cuts off all the oxygen to his brain.

A.J. Carothers

Bad gossip drives out good gossip.

Liz Smith

To put it rather bluntly, I am not the type who wants to go back to the land; I am the type who wants to go back to the hotel.

Fran Lebowitz

As far as I'm concerned, "whom" is a word invented to make everyone sound like a butler.

Calvin Trillin

Taking off my stays at the end of the day makes me happier than anything I know.

Joyce Grenfell

It is generally agreed that "Hello" is an appropriate greeting because if you entered a room and said "Goodbye", it could confuse a lot of people.

Dolph Sharp

If a person offends you and you are in doubt as to whether it was intentional or not, do not resort to extreme measures. Simply watch your chance and hit him with a brick.

Mark Twain

Never lose an opportunity to pump ship.

Arthur Wallesley

Michael Arlen is every other inch a gentleman.

Rebecca West

There is a huge difference between disliking somebody and actually shooting them, strangling them, dragging them through the fields and setting their house on fire. It is that difference which has kept the vast majority of the population of Earth alive today.

Douglas Adams

I beg your pardon for calling on you in this informal manner, but your house is on fire.

Mark Twain

While your friend holds you affectionately by both your hands, you are safe, for you can watch both of his.

Ambrose Bierce

Anybody who is universally popular is bound to be disliked.

Yogi Berra

There is no such thing as a conversation. There are intersecting monologues, that is all.

Rebecca West

During the lunch hour I walked with a friend to a restaurant when we saw lying on the street a helpless fellow human being who had collapsed. Not only had nobody bothered to stop and help this poor fellow, but on our way back after lunch we passed him by still lying in the same spot.

H.L. Mencken

A positive attitude may not solve all your problems, but it will annoy enough people to make it worth the effort.

Herm Albright

It is wrong to discriminate based on skin colour, when there are so many other reasons to dislike someone.

Dennis Miller

It is always a silly thing to give advice, but to give good advice is fatal.

Oscar Wilde

A reputation for wit is earned not by making jokes but by laughing at the pleasantries of others.

Quentin Crisp

Most of the Biddles and Cadwaladers are now either in front of bars or behind bars.

Cleveland Amory

I am one of those unhappy persons who inspires bores to the highest flights of their art.

Edith Sitwell

Lovers of humanity generally hate people and children and keep parrots or puppy dogs.

Roy Campbell

Some cause happiness wherever they go; others whenever they go.

Oscar Wilde

I am very handy with my advice and then when anybody appears to be following it, I get frantic.

Flannery O'Connor

Looking good and dressing well are essential. A purpose in life is not.

Oscar Wilde

I went to a lunch party given by Lady Colefax – the Mother of the Unknown Warrior.

Geoffrey Madan

There is no one I would rather attend a farewell dinner for than Lord Fraser.

R.A. Butler

I went to a party in a large white sheet as Alaska.

Jo Brand

The trouble with Wednesday is that it interferes with both weekends.

Robert Murphy

The trouble with true humility is that you can't talk about it.

Michael Thomsett

Every ten minutes that you delay going to pick up your children from a friend's party erodes your friendship with their parents by one year.

Esther Selsdon

Did you ever notice that no matter what colour shirt you wear, the fluff in your belly button is always the same colour?

Jimeoin McKeown

Never steal anything so small that you'll have to go to an unpleasant city jail instead of a minimum security federal tennis prison.

P. J. O'Rourke

Cherie Blair's hairdressing costs for a trip to the U.S.A. were £2,000. The most expensive haircut I ever had cost ten pounds: and nine pounds went on the search fee.

William Hague

The Duke of Windsor was an extremely dull man. He even danced a boring Charleston, which is no mean feat.

Noel Coward

If things get any worse, I'll have to ask you to stop helping me.

Roseanne Barr

When I saw Swaffer's fingernails, I thanked God I didn't have to look at his feet.

Athene Seyler

There is a lot to say in her favour, but the other is more interesting.

Mark Twain

It's the owners who need to be trained, not the dogs.

Barbara Woodhouse

So great was Bubbles Rothermere's love of parties that she would attend the opening of an envelope.

Christine Hamilton

I hate to see women breastfeeding in public: the baby's head obscures your view.

Sean Meo

A friend is someone who calls at your house even if he doesn't need anything.

C. Buddenleigh

Egotism is the anaesthetic that dulls the pain of stupidity.

Frank Leahy

A thing worth having is a thing worth cheating for.

W.C. Fields

To be positive is to be mistaken at the top of one's voice.

Ambrose Bierce

Lying is the most basic means of self-defence.

Susan Sontag

Peter Sellers was his own worst enemy, although there was lots of competition.

Roy Boulting

Sport

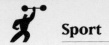

Sport

The problem with hunting, as a sport, is that it is not competitive. A guy with a shotgun squats in a swamp. An unarmed duck with an I.Q. of maybe four flies overhead; the guy blasts the duck into individual duck molecules. Where is the challenge here?

Dave Barry

Women want to be loved, to be listened to, to be desired, to be respected, to be needed, to be trusted, and sometimes, just to be held. Men just want tickets for the World Series.

Dave Barry

They've nicknamed me Ena Sharples because my head was never out of the net.

Ian Thain

Contrary to popular belief, I have always had a wonderful repertoire with my players.

Danny Ozark

Water polo is terribly dangerous. I had two horses drowned under me.

Tony Curtis

What James Dalton lacks in intelligence, he makes up for in stupidity.

Neil Francis

What a game! The referee was wearing glasses over his contact lenses.

Mike Harding

In the opening twenty minutes at Murrayfield, Portugal bought more dummies than a nurse on a maternity ward.

Alasdair Reid

Even though I've retired from boxing, I still go to the gym to spar every day. I miss being hit on the head.

Frank Bruno

Southampton football team is a very well-run outfit from Monday to Friday. It's Saturdays we've got a problem with.

Lawrie McMenemy

In my house in Houston I still have that putter with which I missed that two and a half foot to win the Open. It's in two pieces.

Doug Sanders

Do you know what I love most about baseball? The pine tar, the resin, the grass, the dirt: and that's just in the hot-dogs.

David Letterman

I don't know if the marriage of Joe DiMaggio and Marilyn Monroe is good for baseball but it sure beats the hell out of rooming with Phil Rizzuto.

Yogi Berra

There are only two inevitable things in life: people die and football managers get sacked.

Eoin Hand

Alan Hansen looks like a pissed vampire.

Chris Donald

Our shot-putters are in better condition than Gazza.

Linford Christie

I'm not a believer in luck, although I believe you need it.

Alan Ball

Glen Hoddle has nothing against the disabled. After all, he picked eleven of them to play for England.

Ian Hislop

In Wales's last attack, Scott Quinnell brushed aside three Irish players as if they were mannequins.

Denis Walsh

Football is just a fertility festival. Eleven sperm trying to get into the egg. I feel sorry for the goalkeeper.

Björk

No, of course I haven't been betting on horses Sybil dear. That's just another little avenue of pleasure you've closed off.

Basil Fawlty

Being hit by Victor Costello is like being hit by a cement mixer travelling at forty miles an hour.

George Hook

Women are around all the time but the World Cup comes only once every four years.

Peter Osgood

Kenny Dalglish wasn't that big but he had a huge arse. It came down below his knees and that's where he got his strength from.

Brian Clough

Do my eyes deceive me or is Senna's car sounding a bit rough?

Murray Walker

People seem to think that Jack Charlton and I are exactly the same. But I was a forthright, blunt, arrogant bastard long before I ever got involved with him.

Mick McCarthy

I was watching Germany and I got up to make a cup of tea. I bumped into the telly and Klinsmann fell over.

Frank Skinner

Joe Dimaggio is one of the loneliest guys I ever knew. He leads the league in room service.

Joe E. Brown

I know soccer stories so succulent you would feast on them like Pavarotti at a chophouse after the three-minute warning went off.

Danny Baker

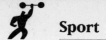

Sport

Bolton Wanderers are doing well aren't they? Last season we got a corner.

Stu Francis

We will definitely improve this year. Last year we lost ten games. This year we play only nine.

Ray Jenkins

The entire contents of the Manchester City trophy room have been stolen. Police are looking for a man carrying a light blue carpet.

Bernard Manning

When I toured with the Irish rugby team I found social contact with other members of the squad very difficult. They were always using big words like "galvanise" and "marmalade".

Phil O'Callaghan

Football is football; if that weren't the case, it wouldn't be the game it is.

Garth Crooks

The Sheffield United strip looks as if it was designed by Julian Cleary when he had a migraine.

Sean Bean

Quit fouling like a wimp. If you're gonna foul, knock the crap outta him.

Norm Stewart

The sport of skiing consists of wearing three thousand dollars' worth of clothes and equipment and driving for two hundred miles in the snow in order to stand around at a bar and get drunk.

P. J. O'Rourke

I'm a great fan of baseball: I watch a lot of games on the radio.

Gerald Ford

Pressure is no excuse for Cantona's behaviour. I would take any amount of personal abuse for £10,000 a week.

Stanley Matthews

If Roger Chase wants to become popular it's easy: he should quit as chairman.

Jimmy Jones

If a woman has to choose between catching a fly ball and saving an infant's life, she will choose to save the infant's life without even considering if there are men on base.

Dave Barry

The most effective way of getting rid of vermin is hunting: provided that a sufficient number of them fall off their horses and break their necks.

Hugh Leonard

If you can't imitate him, don't copy him.

Yogi Berra

Since retiring from riding, eating is going to be a whole new ball game. I may even have to buy a new pair of trousers.

Lester Piggot

Every Monday Stan Collymore would ask me to give him a good boot on the ankle so that he's be injured for Tuesday's training.

Darren Reilly

This is a football. It's an elongated spheroid, inflated with air and covered with an outer layer of coarsely grained leather. Heaven help the first man who fumbles it.

John Heisman

Welcome back to BBC2. While you were away we had a bit of excitement: the batsman asked the umpire if the sightscreen could be moved a few inches to the left and the umpire refused.

Richie Benaud

Golf scores are directly proportional to the number of witnesses.

Robin Wilson

It was grand playing for Nottingham Forest. Brian Clough told me just to go out, get the ball, and give it to my Nigel.

Roy Keane

At one stage I gave up golf and took up ten-pin bowling for a while. At least I didn't lose so many balls.

Bob Hope

It's a pleasure to be standing up here. In fact it's a pleasure to be standing up.

George Best

Boxing got me started on philosophy. You bash them, they bash you and you think, what's it all for?

Arthur Mullard

Football is a very simple game. For ninety minutes, twenty-two men go running after the ball and at the end the Germans win.

Gary Lineker

My favourite event at the Wimbledon Tennis Championships is the mixed singles.

Des MacHale

The other advantage England have got when Phil Tufnell is bowling is that he isn't fielding.

Ian Chappell

My skill at slip is due to the fact that when I was quite young I made a boy, when out for a walk, throw stones into the hedge, and as the sparrows flew out, I caught them.

F. R. Spofforth

As the race wore on, his oar was dipping into the water nearly twice as often as any other.

Desmond Coke

Sport

We don't mind sitting around Wimbledon in the rain waiting for play, but the moment we see Cliff Richard, we're off.

David Stoneball

You can't stay married in a situation where you're afraid to go to sleep in case your wife might cut your throat.

Mike Tyson

A loving wife is better than making fifty at cricket or even ninety-nine; beyond that I will not go.

J. M. Barrie

Who needs the N.F.L. and their stupid "No Taunting" rule? You can hit a guy at full speed and put him in the hospital, but you can't say "Nah, nah! Quarterback has a big butt."

Drew Carey

Professional cricket coaching for women is a man trying to get you to keep your legs close together when other men had spent a lifetime trying to get them apart.

Rachel Heyhoe-Flint

They call it golf because all the other good four-letter words were already taken.

Lewis Grizzard

I've been writing a book for years. It's called *Horses That Owe Me Money*, and I haven't come to the end of it yet.

Sophie Tucker

Whatever you say to the referee, leave his mother out of it.

Jim Davis

The uglier a man's legs are, the better he plays golf. It's almost a law.

H.G.Wells

When you see a cricket coach, run off as fast as you can.

Bill O'Reilly

The last bowler to be knighted was Sir Francis Drake.

Alec Bedser

The Republic of Ireland have just one game plan. If Plan A fails, resort to Plan A.

Mark Lawrenson

Never put superglue in a bowling ball.

Fred Flintstone

Terry Venables has a choice of Gascoigne, Platt, Beardsley and Ince. Any of those would be in the Swiss side. I've got to pick between Sforza, Sforza and Sforza. I usually pick Sforza.

Roy Hodgson

I can bowl so slowly that if I don't like a ball I can run after it and bring it back.

J. M. Barrie

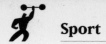

Ballet has always looked to me like football for girls. Both sports exist in a prolonged artificial prepubescence that gives the audience permission to exercise simple primary-playground emotions. Their practitioners remain in a neotenised childhood where bodies are artificially manipulated and the physical, moral and spiritual casualty rate is so high that in any other sphere of life they'd be banned as cruel.

A.A. Gill

As ducks go, that of Such was up there with the best.

Richard Hobson

Sex is a nicer activity than watching football: no nil-nil draws, no offside trap, no cup upsets and you're warm.

Nick Hornby

Derek Randall bats like an octopus with piles.

Matthew Engel

Alexi Lalas resembles the love child of Rasputin and Phyllis Diller.

Simon Ingram

The Bolivian football team leave me as baffled as Adam on Mother's Day.

Xavier Azkargorta

Ian Botham couldn't bowl a hoop downhill.

Fred Trueman

Wimbledon have changed their style. They are now kicking the ball fifty yards instead of sixty.

Mike Walker

When I lost the decathlon record, I took it like a man. I cried for a week.

Daley Thompson

The Duke of York got on very badly at Wimbledon. He was left-handed and the crowd tried to encourage him by calling out, "Try the other hand, sir."

Frank Pakenham

The mincing run-up of Merv Hughes resembles someone in high heels and a panty girdle chasing after a bus.

Martin Johnson

The only thing Ian Botham knows about dawn runs is coming back from parties.

Graham Gooch

Real golfers don't cry when they line up their fourth putt.

Karen Hurwitz

Confidence builds with successive putts. The putter, then, is a club designed to hit the ball partway to the hole.

Ring Lardner

Real golfers tape the Masters so they can go play themselves.

George Roope

Golf is a typical capitalist lunacy of upper-class Edwardian England.

George Bernard Shaw

The noise that comes from the wretched throats of a boxing crowd indicates that brain damage is also in the head of the beholder.

Julie Burchill

I missed a three-inch putt to lose the Oakland Open by one shot. I've got a hen back home that can lay an egg further than that.

Clayton Heafner

Nicklaus was only five strokes back. I wouldn't feel safe from Jack if he was in a wheelchair.

Dan Jenkins

My wife prepares her golf bag as if when we are playing the fourteenth hole, World War III will break out and we will spend at least twelve months living in a bunker. Therefore in addition to a full set of golf clubs, the bag contains a survival kit of sweets, various nibbles, a flask of tea, bottles of mineral water, insect repellents, sun cream, elastoplasts, tropical clothing, thermal underwear, thick sweaters, and a complete set of waterproofs in case she has to be rescued by a lifeboat.

Michael Parkinson

The only time I ever took out a one-iron was to kill a tarantula. And I took a seven to do that.

Jim Murray

I tee the ball high because through the years of experience I have found that the air offers less resistance than dirt.

Jack Nicklaus

Bobby Peel was regularly inebriated during cricket matches and often drank himself into a state tactfully referred to in Wisden as "unwell" or "gone away". During one county game he was suspended for "running the wrong way" and "bowling at the pavilion in the belief that it was the batsman".

Karl Shaw

My three playing partners drove into the woods. I asked them what was over there, a nudist colony?

Lee Trevino

The word "aerobics" come from two Greek words: "aero", meaning "ability to" and "bics" meaning "withstand tremendous boredom".

Dave Barry

I found an old swimming suit that I had made out of sponges. I remember one time I wore it in the pool, then I left and nobody could go swimming until I came back.

Steven Wright

Atherton lacks that one vital ingredient an English captain needs to survive: miracles.

Graham Gooch

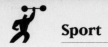

Sport

Boxing is just show business with blood.

Frank Bruno

We sometimes argue about the cricketer we would choose to bat for one's life (consensus answer: Don Bradshaw for your life, Geoff Boycott for his own).

Matthew Engel

Golf is a dull game. The players are dull robots carrying sticks. They don't even spit or scratch their privates like other athletes.

Lewis Grizzard

Paul Gascoigne is Tyneside's very own Renaissance man. A man capable of breaking both leg and wind at the same time.

Jimmy Greaves

There are over a hundred and fifty golf courses in the Palm Springs area and Jerry Ford is never sure which one he's going to play until his second shot.

Bob Hope

I prefer cricket to baseball; I don't think I can be expected to take seriously any game which takes less than three days to reach its conclusion.

Tom Stoppard

Cricket is just organised loafing.

Peter West

He asked me what time it was and I asked him, "You mean now?"

Yogi Berra

The difference between John Hart and an arsonist is that an arsonist doesn't throw away his last two matches.

Brent Pope

Alan Shepard walking on the moon found a golf ball with Gerald Ford's initials on it.

Bob Hope

You can make basketball more exciting by eliminating the referees, raising the basket four feet, doubling the size of the basketball, limiting the height of the players to five foot nine inches, bringing back the centre jump, allowing taxi drivers in free and allowing players to carry guns.

Al McGuire

I used to go missing a lot: Miss Canada, Miss United Kingdom, Miss World.

George Best

I took one look at my opponent in the boxing ring and said to the referee, "I'm not fighting until I hear it tork!"

Spike Milligan

I've told the players we need to win so that I can have cash to buy some new ones.

Chris Turner

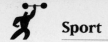 **Sport**

Players of virtual reality football should remember that, as with all sports, it is important to warm up properly and wear appropriate footwear.

Graham Tytherleigh-Strong

So the concussed striker doesn't know who he is. Tell him he's Pele and put him back on.

John Lambie

If we played like that every week we wouldn't be inconsistent.

Bryan Robson

Defensively, the Red Sox are a lot like Stonehenge. They are old, they don't move and no one is certain why they are positioned the way they are.

Dan Shaughnessy

"Clinical" is an adjective used by football commentators to show that they can handle three-syllable words.

Michael O'Donnell

Baseball is supposed to be a non-contact sport, but our hitters seem to be taking that literally.

Larry Doughty

The Pittsburgh Pirates have a worse defence than Pearl Harbor.

Andy Van Slyke

I'd hang myself, but Hamilton Academicals cannot afford the rope.

Iain Munro

The ball is man's most disastrous invention, not excluding the wheel.

Robert Morley

Referees should be wired up to a couple of electrodes and they should be allowed three mistakes before you run 50,000 volts through their genitals.

John Gregory

I remember when Steve Davis used to take Valium as a stimulant.

Denis Taylor

Theatre and Criticism

For a man linked with satire, Peter Cook was without malice to anyone, although he did admit to pursuing an irrational vendetta against the late great Gracie Fields.

Richard Ingrams

There was a vaudeville actor who died and left an estate of eight hundred hotel and Pullman towels.

W. C. Fields

Ballet means paying a lot of money just to see buggers jump.

Nigel Bruce

My performance in *Hamlet* was not as bad as the critics claimed. I neither waved to my friends in the audience nor walked through the scenery.

Kenneth Tynan

Demi Moore's breasts hang around *Striptease* like a couple of silicon albatrosses.

Mark Steyn

Acting is merely the expression of a neurotic impulse. It's a bum's life. The principal benefit acting has afforded me is the money to pay for my psychoanalysis.

Marlon Brando

I was planning to go into architecture, but when I arrived at college registration, architecture was filled up. Acting was right next to it, so I signed up for acting instead.

Tom Selleck

Lillian Gish may be a charming person, but she is not
Ophelia. She comes on stage as if she had been sent out for
to sew rings on the new curtains.

Mrs. Patrick Campbell

Jamie Lee Curtis has trouble learning her lines because
English is not her first language. She doesn't, unfortunately,
have a first language.

John Cleese

Those big empty houses do not scare me: I was in vaudeville.

Bob Hope

Never forget what I am going to tell you: actors are crap.

John Ford

An actor who drinks is in a bad way; but the actor who eats
is lost.

George Bernard Shaw

Godspell is back in London. For those who missed it the first
time, this is a golden opportunity to miss it again.

Michael Billington

I'm glad you liked my portrayal of Catherine the Great. I
like her too. She ruled over thirty million people and had
three thousand lovers. I do the best I can in two hours.

Mae West

Sean Connery has such a deep love of Scotland that he refuses to use anything other than a Scottish accent no matter what the role he is taking.

Graham Norton

Borstal Boy is a show that will run on and on like a gurrier's nosebleed.

Hugh Leonard

Dying is easy. Comedy is hard.

Edmund Gwenn

When I get hold of Bette Davis, I will tear every hair out of her moustache.

Tallulah Bankhead

I was on tour with a review that played the Palace at Westcliff-on-Sea in Essex; the review in the local paper was headlined, "Another nail in the Palace coffin".

Roy Hudd

Roman Polanski is the five-foot Pole you wouldn't want to touch anyone with.

Kenneth Tynan

The promoters of the new technology say that this marks the first time that an entertainer who is no longer living has headlined a concert. Oh really? Have they never seen the Royal Variety Performance?

Richard Morrison

To say that Michael Winner is his own worst enemy is to provoke a ragged chorus from odd corners of the film industry of "Not while I'm alive."

Barry Norman

God was very good to the world when He took Miriam Hopkins from us.

Bette Davis

The word agent is the most disgusting word in the English language.

Peggy Ramsay

Rod Hull is a man who spends his evenings with his arm up a tatty old bird.

Paul Merton

The most famous building in the heart of Dublin is the architecturally undistinguished Abbey Theatre, once the city morgue and now entirely restored to its original purpose.

Frank O'Connor

Once seen, Walter Matthau's antique-mapped face is never forgotten: a bloodhound with a head cold, a man who is simultaneously biting on a bad lobster and caught by the neck in lift doors, a mad scientist's amalgam of Wallace Beer and Yogi Bear.

Alan Brien

Frank Rich and John Simon are the syphilis and gonorrhoea of the theatre.

David Mamet

Marilyn Monroe is a broad with a future behind her.

Constance Bennett

When I look back, the fondest memory I have is not really of the Goons. It is of a girl called Julia with enormous breasts.

Spike Milligan

If Rice Krispies could talk, they would sound like Barbra Streisand.

John Simon

My name was in large type, right across the bottom of the bill declaring that I was "The Popular Comedian!" The first bill I saw displayed on a hoarding was so close to the ground that the local dogs had already given their opinion of me.

Arthur Askey

I have never written for the intelligentsia. Sixteen curtain calls and closed on Saturday.

Noel Coward

He directed *Charlie's Aunt* with all the airy deftness of a rheumatic deacon producing *Macbeth* for a church social.

Noel Coward

Tallulah Bankhead is a marvellous female impersonator.

Anne Baxter

Descriptions of my face have included comparisons with most root vegetables.

Frankie Howerd

This Was A Man made *Parsifal* in its entirety seem like a quick-fire vaudeville sketch.

Noel Coward

Marlene Dietrich has sex without gender.

Kenneth Tynan

I like to be introduced as America's foremost actor. It saves the necessity of further effort.

John Barrymore

A. E. Matthews ambled through *This Was A Man* like a charming retriever who has buried a bone and can't quite remember where.

Noel Coward

The opening night of a play is the night before the play is ready to open.

George Nathan

The show closed like a tired clam.

W. C. Fields

Alec Guinness is an actor who plays by himself to himself. In *The Scapegoat* he plays a dual role, so at least he was able to play with himself.

Bette Davis

I was a sort of Vanessa Redgrave of the fifties.

Peter O'Toole

Until Ace Ventura, no actor had considered talking through his ass.

Jim Carrey

The tights on the male dancers were so tight you could tell what religion they were.

Robin Williams

Kissing Woody Allen was like kissing the Berlin Wall.

Helena Bonham Carter

The box office is the only truly romantic part of the theatre.

Peggy Ramsay

Camelot is about as long as *Parsifal*, and not as funny.

Noel Coward

Cary Grant needed willowy or boyish girls like Katharine Hepburn to make him look macho. If I'd co-starred with Grant I'd have eaten him for breakfast.

Bette Davis

Orson Welles was clad in a black barrage balloon cleverly painted to look like a dinner jacket.

Clive James

Full-frontal nudity has now become accepted by every branch of the theatrical profession with the possible exception of lady accordion players.

Denis Norden

Diana Ross walks into a pool hall and they chalk her head.

Joan Rivers

Humphrey Bogart's performance in *Swifty* was what is usually described and mercifully described as inadequate.

Alexander Woollcott

The theatre is a profession in which immense hits may never be repeated and, indeed, may be followed by a series of flops. Authors as well as playwrights enjoy it for the same reason that a person gets pleasure out of pressing one's tongue against a sore throat.

Hugh Rawson

I remember a landlady who used to split her dining room into two halves: straight actors on the left, variety turns to the right.

Ernie Wise

Ladies, just a little more virginity, if you don't mind.

Herbert Beerbohm Tree

I submit all my plays to the National Theatre for rejection to assure myself I am seeing clearly.

Howard Barker

I never did the man an injury, yet the actor Henderson would read his tragedy to me.

Samuel Johnson

There are three types of actress: the silly, the very silly and Shirley MacLaine.

P. J. O'Rourke

Dear boy, good wasn't the word for your performance.

Noel Coward

Are you ready backstage? Then release the goats.

Ken Dodd

I don't care what the others say about you, darling, I thought you were wonderful.

Coral Browne

Ballet: I can think of nothing more kinky than a prince chasing a swan around all night.

Robert Helpmann

The first night of *Peter Pan*: oh, for an hour of Herod.

Anthony Hope

Phoebe Lucas would play a glamorous courtesan with about as much sex appeal as a haddock.

Noel Coward

I approach reading reviews the way some people anticipate anal warts.

Roseanne Barr

I thought they said "omelette" and since I was really hungry I nodded. I wound up playing Hamlet.

Paul Gross

At last it was over, and the theatre rang with the grateful applause of the released.

Edith Wharton

Those whom God wishes to punish He makes mad. Then He gives them an equity card.

Donal McCann

I believe that God felt sorry for actors so He created Hollywood to give them a place in the sun and a swimming pool. The price they had to pay was to surrender their talent.

Cedric Hardwicke

The fashion for nudity will never extend to dance, because there are portions of the human anatomy which would keep swinging after the music had finished.

Robert Helpmann

Acting is merely the art of keeping a large number of people from coughing.

Ralph Richardson

Bruce Lee was a psychopathic Michael Flatley.

A.A. Gill

I was bold enough to decline an invitation to *Hamlet* on the grounds that I already knew who won.

Quentin Crisp

Jennifer Saunders is a one-trick horse; Dawn French is a one-trick carthorse.

A.A. Gill

Laurence Olivier is the most overrated actor on earth. Take away the wives and the looks and you have John Gielgud.

Oscar Levant

Mae West's Catherine the Great is going to be a bust, which will give Miss West one more than she needs.

John Chapman

During the opening of *Hamlet* in New York, I delivered the "To be or not to be" speech in German. Nobody – the director, the stage manager or the audience – seemed to notice it.

Richard Burton

Gary Cooper had two emotions: "hat on" and "hat off".

Niall Toibin

I want the cast to stop acting and get on with the play.

Sam Goldwyn

You can have them rolling in the aisles with a joke in Glasgow and it won't get a laugh in Manchester. Because they can't hear it.

Ken Dodd

In Milwaukee last month a man died, laughing at one of his own jokes. That's what makes it so tough for us outsiders. We have to fight home competition.

Robert Benchley

I was doing a comedy gig in a club in Aberdeen three weeks ago and I went out for a few minutes. When I came back the place was a supermarket.

Frank Carson

You can make a sordid thing sound like a brilliant drawing-room comedy. Probably a fear of facing up to the real issues. Could you say we are guilty of Noel Cowardice?

Peter De Vries

Madonna is a gay man trapped in a woman's body.

George O'Dowd

Mrs. Patrick Campbell was like a sinking ship firing on the rescuers.

Alexander Woollcott

What little weight Ally McBeal has appears to be in her fillings.

Caitlin Moran

With his mellifluously mannered diction and his gaunt-yet-loopy good looks, Richard E. Grant always plays the same basic character, simply varying the degree of intensity with which he rolls his eyeballs.

Paul Hoggart

Acting with him was like acting with 210 pounds of condemned veal.

Coral Browne

For God's sake go and tell that young man to take that Rockingham tea service out of his tights.

Noel Coward

I never read bad reviews about myself because my best friends invariably tell me about them.

Oscar Levant

The only way this actress will get her name into the *New York Times* is if somebody shoots her.

George Kaufman

Good taste would likely have the same effect on Howard Stern that daylight has on Dracula.

Ted Koppel

Pantomime is the smell of oranges and wee-wee.

Arthur Askey

"Critic" is a six-letter word for a four-letter concept.

Piers Anthony

Geoffrey Palmer plays comedy sadly, as if his canary has just died.

Hugh Leonard

The Royal Shakespeare Company once did *Julius Caesar* in New York. When Caesar was stabbed onstage, half the audience left because they didn't want to get involved.

Bob Monkhouse

That actress wouldn't get a laugh if she pulled a kipper out of her ★★★★.

Noel Coward

Miscellaneous

The main quality for membership of Brook's Club Library Committee would appear to be illiteracy qualified by absenteeism.

Geoffrey Madan

Members of the public committing suicide from the 140-foot tower on my estate do so at their own risk.

Gerald Tyrwhitt-Wilson

Dancing with her was like moving a piano.

Ring Lardner

She was beheaded, chopped into pieces and placed in a trunk, but she was not interfered with.

Nick Reaney

The committee will be composed of open-minded people who agree with me.

Edward McKita

Have you ever noticed how anybody going slower than you is an idiot while anybody going faster than you is a maniac?

George Carlin

You know you've made the wrong decision when the notice advertising vacancies is screwed to the front gate of the hotel.

Pat Blackford

I refuse to travel on any airline where the pilots believe in reincarnation.

Spalding Gray

I had all the spots removed from my dice for luck, but I remember where they formerly were.

Damon Runyon

Some of my jokes would make rhubarb grow.

Roy Brown

I have a warm place for you Charles; not in my heart, in my fireplace.

W. C. Fields

The worst bit of gossip I ever heard about myself was that I was having a gay affair with Arthur Mullard.

Roy Hudd

At no time is freedom of speech more precious than when a man hits his thumb with a hammer.

Marshall Lumsden

He was madder than Mad Jack McMad, winner of last year's madman contest.

Rowan Atkinson

This car can turn on a sixpence: whatever that is.

Nubar Gulbenkian

Prussian Field Marshal Prince Gebhard Leberecht von
Blucher, whose timely intervention sealed Wellington's
triumph at Waterloo, was convinced that he was pregnant
with an elephant, fathered on him by a French soldier.

Geoff Tibballs

The sign said, "This door is not to be used as an entrance or
an exit."

Gerald Hazzard

Sleep is like death without the long-term commitment.

Lea Krinsky

Don't worry about the world ending today: it's already
tomorrow in Australia.

Steven Wright

I was hitchhiking the other day and a hearse stopped. I said
"No thanks, I'm not going that far."

Steven Wright

I have seen better organised creatures than you running
around farmyards with their heads cut off.

John Cleese

My wife came home and said she had some good news and
some bad news about the car. I said, "What's the good
news?" She said, "The airbag works."

Roy Brown

The early bird may get the worm, but the second mouse gets the cheese.

Steven Wright

Any walk through a park that runs between a double line of mangy trees by the ladies' toilet is invariably known as "Lovers' Lane".

F. Scott Fitzgerald

I landed at Orly airport and discovered my luggage wasn't on the same plane. My bags were finally traced to Israel where they were opened and all my trousers were altered.

Woody Allen

Public transport should be avoided with exactly the same zeal that one accords to the avoidance of Herpes II.

Fran Lebowitz

If the remarks with which I am credited and never made are really good, I acknowledge them. I generally work myself into the belief that I originally said them.

Noel Coward

In the city a funeral is just a traffic obstruction; in the country it is a form of entertainment.

George Ade

Experience teaches that it doesn't.

Norman McCaig

World War Two wasn't good for much except for destroying Hitler and furthering Vera Lynn's career.

Alexei Sayle

When you have got an elephant by the hind leg, and he is trying to run away, it is best to let him run.

Abraham Lincoln

Hate mail is the only kind of letter that never gets lost by the Post Office.

Philip Kerr

You don't need to use a sledgehammer to crack a walnut, but it's a lot of fun trying.

Graham Keith

I'm a hero with coward's legs.

Spike Milligan

Show me a man with both feet on the ground and I'll show you a man who cannot put his pants on.

Arthur Watson

When just about everything is coming your way, you're obviously in the wrong lane.

Michael Caine

Nostalgia ain't what it used to be.

Yogi Berra

My last comment on leaving the Titanic was, "I rang for ice, but this is ridiculous."

Madeline Astor

Whenever I think of the past, it brings back so many memories.

Steven Wright

Eleven men well armed will certainly subdue one single man in his shirt.

Jonathan Swift

As the horsepower in modern automobiles steadily rises, the congestion of traffic steadily lowers the possible speed of your car. This is known as Progress.

Sydney J. Harris

The future ain't what it used to be.

Yogi Berra

Cavalry should be used in modern warfare to add a little tone to what would otherwise be a vulgar brawl.

Richard Winward

I knew I was going to take the wrong train, so I left early.

Yogi Berra

The most stupid thing I ever did was to put a knife in the fork drawer.

Bob Mortimer

I am not superstitious but I would not sleep thirteen to a bed on a Friday night.

Chauncey Depew

My grandfather fought in the First World War. He was shot in the Dardanelles: very painful.

Frankie Howerd

An unbiased opinion is always absolutely valueless.

Oscar Wilde

What is yellow and lies at the bottom of the Atlantic Ocean? Sand!

Rick Mayall

I am not arguing with you: I am telling you.

James McNeill Whistler

I wear a zebra: that's twenty-six sizes larger than an A bra.

Jo Brand

We are not retreating, merely advancing in another direction.

Douglas Adams

Garden catalogues are as big liars as house agents.

Rumer Godden

"Fragile" is usually interpreted by postal workers as "please throw underarm".

Morey Amsterdam

It is truth you cannot contradict; you can without any difficulty contradict Socrates.

Plato

In Connecticut, a prisoner on death row has gone on hunger strike. Now there's a problem that pretty much takes care of itself.

Jay Leno

He who lives by the sword will eventually be wiped out by some bastard with a sawn-off shotgun.

Steady Eddy

Club 18–30 holidays: you know they're referring to I.Q. there, don't you?

Ben Elton

The other day I... No, that wasn't me.

Steven Wright

I am confused as a baby in a topless bar.

Betty Black

You can't learn too soon that the most useful thing about a principle is that it can always be sacrificed to expediency.

Somerset Maugham

Miscellaneous

A doorman is a genius who can open the door of your car with one hand, help you in with the other, and still have one left for the tip.

Dorothy Kilgallen

Cab drivers are living proof that practice does not make perfect.

Howard Ogden

The quietest place in the world is the complaint department at the parachute packing plant.

Jackie Martling

Airline hostesses show you how to use a seat belt in case you haven't been in a car since 1965.

Jerry Seinfeld

There is only one thing about which I am certain and that is that there is nothing about which one can be certain.

Somerset Maugham

Never approach a bull from the front, a horse from the rear or a fool from any direction.

Ken Alstad

I was reading in this book that the first tube station ever opened was Baker Street in 1863. What was the point of that? Where would you go?

Paul Merton

I went into the hardware store and bought some used paint.
It was in the shape of a house.

Steven Wright

He called me a fatalist, but I'd never collected a postage
stamp in my life.

Yogi Berra

The most difficult things for a man to do are to climb a wall
leaning towards you, to kiss a girl leaning away from you, and
to make an after-dinner speech.

Winston Churchill

I pray that there's intelligent life somewhere out there in
space because there's bugger all down here on earth.

Eric Idle

All cats should be muzzled outside to stop the agonising
torture of mice and small birds.

Viscount Monckton

The Devil himself has probably redesigned Hell in the light
of information he has gained from observing airport layouts.

Anthony Price

My daughter was tragically abducted by wombats.

Edna Everage

The only lie that Moore ever told was when I asked him if he always spoke the truth and he replied, "No".

Bertrand Russell

A prisoner of war is someone who tries to kill you, fails, and then asks you not to kill him.

Winston Churchill

Whenever I put anything smart on, for some reason, within seconds, a portion of meat curry will fly through the air on to my chest.

Jo Brand

Why do we step in dog dirt? You don't see dogs stepping in dog dirt.

Jimeoin McKeown

When it comes to giving to others, I stop at nothing.

Roger Price

I found it ironic to hear the Queen reading her speech about abolishing fox hunting to Parliament with a dead stoat wrapped around her neck. But that's not a nice way to talk about the Duke of Edinburgh.

Paul Merton

The word DUCK is seventy-five per cent obscene.

Lenny Bruce

Miscellaneous

If you're famous never wear suede shoes. Because if you do, somebody will be standing next to you in the gents and will turn towards you and say, "Hey, it's John Wayne!" and he will pee all over your shoes. With leather, it's not too bad but it ruins suede.

John Wayne

Field Marshal Alexander was a perfect soldier and a perfect gentleman. He never gave offence to anyone, not even the enemy.

A. J. P. Taylor

Index

Index

Index

Index

Index